MEDIEVAL JEWISH MYSTICISM

BOOK OF THE PIOUS

Sholom Alchanan Singer

Publishers/WHITEHALL COMPANY
601 Skokie Blvd./Northbrook, Ill.

In memory of my father, Zevulon,
who taught me love of wisdom.

In honor of my mother, Miriam,
who taught me the wisdom of love.

ACKNOWLEDGEMENTS

This work has been a shared one. Many friends, teachers and loved ones must be thanked for their kindness and help in enabling me to complete this study.

My appreciation to Dr. O.J.M. Jolles, formerly Chairman of the Committee of the History of Culture at the University of Chicago, who initiated and supervised this project.

Appreciation, too, for the guidance and encouragement of my teacher, Dr. James Lea Cate, Professor Emeritus of Medieval History at the University of Chicago for whose friendship I am deeply grateful.

If the reader finds any merit or fluency in this volume it is due in large measure to the example set by Dr. Theodore Silverstein, Professor of English and Medieval Studies at the University of Chicago. It is my hope that his wide erudition, eloquence and painstaking care have been reflected throughout this book.

To Dr. Judah Rosenthal, Professor Emeritus of Biblical Exegesis and Codes of the College of Jewish Studies, Chicago, Illinois, whose dedicated scholarship I have been privileged to know, I am deeply beholden for the love and vast scholarly resources he brought to this work. Each paragraph and phrase received his lavish attention and meticulous concern.

To my colleague Dr. Edgar Siskin, rabbi of North Shore Congregation Israel, Glencoe, Illinois, gratitude for his friendship and counsel and for his admirable example of integrity and kindness.

Heartfelt thanks to my congregation B'nai Torah of Highland Park, Illinois for the understanding which enables me to fulfill the classic function of the rabbinate, to study, to teach and write.

Finally, to my devoted wife, Vivian, whose patience and love continues to mystify me, my thanks for all the preparations, indices and details that only deepest affection can infuse with dedication and devotion.

To all who shared in this work I say:

"for from thee is all, and out of thy hand do I return it to thee."

Sholom A. Singer

CONTENTS

INTRODUCTION

The rise of Hasidism in the life of German Jewry has long been regarded as one of the major events in the religious history of that community. For many scholars it is indeed the only decisive development of major consequence in the spiritual life of German Jewry.[1]

This particular religious growth which bears the name *Ha-Hasiduth Ha-Ashkenazith,* German Pietism, evolved under the impact of the crusades and their concomitant persecutions. In essence such newborn pietism represents a response to the methodical pattern of humiliation and degradation inflicted upon Jews during the twelfth and thirteenth centuries; it is a heightened and more intense form of religio-moral idealism and saintliness. Destined to write a glorious chapter in Jewish history, it arose first in the Rhenish Jewish communities. Its representatives were referred to by their contemporaries as *Haside Ashkenaz,* The Devout of Germany.

The creative period of the movement was relatively short, the century from about 1150 to 1250, but its influence on German Jewry was lasting. The religious concepts and ideas to which it gave rise and filled with meaning through their own practice and conduct retained their vitality for centuries.[2] The protagonists of this heightened pietism were accepted and regarded as genuine representatives of an ideal Jewish way of life.

While it is true that the movement itself never achieved the proportions or dimensions of a mass movement, the teachings and leadership did enjoy wide popularity, authority, and prestige. It must, of course, be recognized that the very nature of the calling with its demanding and exacting teachings made it a vocation for the few rather than for the multitude. Nevertheless, it did not preclude the community at large from aspiring to inclusion in its select ranks and being numbered among its devotees. The simple fact that this movement exerted such a powerful influence over a short period of time and a lasting influence over succeeding centuries demonstrates and reveals the deep roots it struck in the heart, life, and mind of German Jewry.

THE TIMES

The settlement of Jews on German soil can be traced back to Roman times. A decree issued by the Emperor Constantine in 321 A.D. explicitly mentions Jews as Roman citizens in Cologne.[3] In all probability Mayence and Treves also saw Jewish settlers in Roman times. The same may be assumed of other communities near the Rhine and Meuse, as well as for other sites along the Danube, for example, Augsburg, Regensburg and the region of Vienna.[4]

Even with the barbarian incursions and the gradual dissolution of Roman hegemony, Jews continued to live in the confines of the later Roman Empire until the time of Charlemagne. During his reign, Jews appear as immigrants following the commercial highways and the civilizing thrusts of cultural proliferation and development. The important trade routes stretching along the Rhine and the Moselle leading to the Danube and into eastern Europe received their share of Jewish merchants. Many settled permanently in these regions. With the emergence of the German cities in the tenth and eleventh centuries many Jews settled in urban centers. This in part was due to efforts made by the founders of these cities to attract Jews, such as, the favors granted them in the famous charter of Bishop Rüdiger of Speyer in 1084.[5] A large network of Jewish communities rose soon after to commercial importance and cultural reknown. Were it not for the havoc sown by the crusades, their achievement would have been even more significant and lasting.

The crusades did much to disrupt, retard and destroy Jewish life in these communities, nevertheless, they endured. While the Jewish spirit was sorely tried and shaken by the destructive and wanton fury of the crusades, it remained unbroken. In many ways the year 1096, which ushered in the age of the crusades, marked a turning point in Jewish history. First, it brought home to the Jews and to their foes alike the utter instability of the Jewish position in the Western world. What had until now been sporadic outbreaks and incidents of a local nature, became concerted actions of widespread dimension. A mass psychosis, transcending national boundaries and directly sanctioning anti-Jewish persecution, blanketed a continent with its contagious appeal. Actually, the events of 1096, when seen in retrospect, appear as the culmination of anti-Jewish trends building up among the Western masses over several generations.[6] Unfortunately, these hostile manifestations were so unrelated chronologically, causally and geographically, that their true portents could not be accurately evaluated even by the most cautious and astute leadership of the day. News of tragedy and terror within the Jewish community moved slowly. Communication with outlying Jewish communities was poor; outbreaks were soon forgotten, and in certain instances the causes were discounted, as largely accidental. This served to obscure the tragic fate in store for the Jews, a fate toward which all events were converging. The crusades not only exacted a toll in human life through massacre and rapine, but also left deep scars in Judeo-Christian relations by setting a very low evaluation on Jewish life and property. Count Emico, who murdered and plundered Jews in the Rhineland towns, was a representative of this new tradition. His actions signaled the beginning of an epoch of terrifying and fanatical brutality toward the Jew.[7] Tragically, some of the most fruitfully rich and creative communities were among those singled out for destruction at the hands of the crusaders. The first and second crusades dealt crushing blows at Speyer, Mayence and Worms. The three crusades that took place within a century, 1096, 1144 and 1189, served another ignominious purpose. Generally, all three crusades conspired to underscore and reinforce the new pattern of degradation imposed upon the Jews. This new pattern manifested itself in economic, social and religious spheres.

The Jew was forced into new avenues of economic activity. His opportunity within commerce became exceedingly limited. Agriculture was already closed to him. One could suggest quite correctly that this change in the economic activity of the Jew came about as a result of a new constellation of circumstances brought on in part by the crusades and the revival of commerce. Commercial traffic was reopened between East and West with dire consequences for Jewish interests. Italian merchant republics, especially Venice, Pisa and Genoa, were strengthened economically as a result of these crusades, and this helped greatly to push Jews out of commerce.

By the end of the eleventh century one may say that the Mediterranean had been reconquered for Christian navigation and commerce between distant parts was entirely in the hands of Westerners.

Thus the crusades completed the process of substituting Christian merchants for Jewish ones. This resulted from the fact that Christians had opened a route to the East.[8]

Needless to say, the periodic crusading eruptions went far toward making it unsafe for Jewish merchants to travel the commercial highways. This contributed to the disruption and diminution of Jewish capital and enterprise. Guilds, operating as closed corporations, made artisan endeavor most difficult for the Jew. Thus, a majority of Jews derived their living from the few petty trades and artisan enterprises that remained open to them. Perhaps the most important economic activity they engaged in during this period was money-lending. In time, this would serve to strengthen the stereotype of the Jew as a commercial oppressor and exploiter of his fellow Christians.[9]

During the twelfth and thirteenth centuries, the Jew achieved a new status in the socio-economic context of the period. His condition was one of isolation and persecution, aptly characterized as the Age of Degradation. The most compelling factor driving the Jew towards "pariah marginality" was his utter exclusion from the great design of the *respublica Christiana*. In this new socio-religious integration, the Jew had no place.[10]

These were not the only tensions, however, experienced by the Jew at this time. There was the presence and pressure of the Church, which intensified his alienation. The supremacy enjoyed by the Church during these centuries led to the characterization of this period as the Age of Papal-Caesarism. The term reflects the realities of the time, the dominance and incomparable prestige of the Catholic Church. It reached its zenith during the pontificate of Innocent III (1198-1216) and his successors, Honorious III, Gregory IX and Innocent IV (1243-1254).

Innocent III formulated the Church's attitude and policy towards Jews. It was stern and oppressive. He urged Christian rulers to exercise their power so that, "Jews will not dare to raise their necks, bowed under the yoke of perpetual slavery, against the reverence of the Christian faith."[11]

German-Jewish pietism emerged from this new configuration of historic forces and circumstances. Emphasis on greater piety and purity in the sight of God had to compensate the Jew for the loss of esteem in the eyes of fellow Christians. Heightened religious enthusiasm and total immersion into punctilious concern for ritual and cultic matters created a buffer for an oppressive and often unbearable reality.

THE MAN

Judah ben Samuel, the Pious of Regensburg (Ratisbon) who is regarded as one of the most prominent and influential of the *Haside Ashkenaz,* the Devout of Germany, was born in Speyer[12] about the year 1140.[13] He died in Regensburg on February 22, 1217.[14] So long as Hasidism remained a living and vital force he held an almost unrivaled position of leadership. There can be no question that his own stature was enhanced by the fact that he was a descendant of one of the most illustrious families in Jewry, the Kalonymides. For many generations his family took a leading part in the development of Jewish learning in Germany.[15] Although originally from Lucca, Italy, the family migrated to many different regions in Europe. A branch of the Kolonymides settled in Speyer, Mayence, and Worms.

Judah the Pious' grandfather, Kalonymus ben Isaac the Elder, already lived in Speyer during the eleventh and twelfth century and established a reputation as rabbi and halakhist. His son Samuel the Pious, the father of Judah, added further to the lustre of the family name through his writings, scholarship, and personal piety.[16] It is, however, unfortunate that most of his writings, which were considerable, have been lost.

Samuel the Pious, his son Judah, and the latter's disciple and relative Eleazar ben Judah of Worms may be regarded as the molders of German Hasidism.[17] The fact that scholarship still remains divided on the question of authorship for the opening sections of *Sefer Hasidim* between Judah, or his father Samuel, reveals the great similarity of ideology and teaching of these two men.[18] Judah the Pious and his brother, Abraham,[19] who was head of an academy in Speyer, were apparently pupils of their father Samuel and received their early instruction from him.[20]

Records indicate that Samuel the Pious was an outstanding Talmudic scholar for his time, in addition to being a pietist of distinction. He maintained an academy in Speyer, wrote commentaries and other works, and is quoted often by contemporary scholars.[21] As far as legend guides us, it seems that Abraham studied with his father Samuel in the conventional and customary setting of student-teacher relationship. Judah's introduction to study was apparently delayed for many years because of his interest in more worldly matters. When he finally began to study, the moment of initiation reverberated with dramatic and prophetic effects,[22] pointing to the fact that Judah would soon overshadow his brother Abraham in mystical knowledge and achievement. After this, Judah applied himself diligently to study.

Later, Judah went to Regensburg,[23] established his dwelling there and was esteemed as one of the foremost scholars and teachers in that town. He wrote many mystical and ethical treatises, the best known being *Sefer Hasidim.*[24] He wrote a commentary on the Pentateuch and books on legalistic matters. Few of these have survived. He was the teacher of Rabbi Eleazar, author of the *Rokeah,* and his mentor in mysticism.

Rabbi Isaac Or Zarua was another of Judah's pupils. A correspondence was carried on between Rabbi Judah and many of the outstanding Franco-German scholars of the day. Rabbi Judah had three sons, Rabbi Samuel, Rabbi Zalman, and Rabbi Moses.[25]

Numerous and illustrious teachers contributed to the personality and development of Rabbi Judah the Pious. Aside from the instruction which Rabbi Judah received from his father in traditional matters, he received his mystical initiation from him as well.[26] The meaning of the "Pyut" he learned from the martyred Rabbi Jom Tob the Holy.[27] He, in turn, influenced very many important rabbis, most especially Rabbi Eleazar b. Judah, called the "Rokeah," Rabbi Baruch of Mayence, Rabbi Isaac Or Zarua. Judah the Pious was referred to by his contemporaries as the "Great Pietist," "Father of Wisdom," and the like.

Legends about Judah abound but their reliability is doubtful.[28] However, through them all there shines the unquestionable impressiveness of his piety and holiness. Tradition states, "If he had lived in the time of the prophets he would surely have been a prophet, if during the time of the Tanaaim a Tana, and in the time of the Amoraim an Amora."[29] His contribution to medieval Jewish mysticism is a matter still to be investigated and evaluated fully.

Part of the difficulty of such an investigation stems from the lack of authentic and reliable primary material dealing with the period. Though the life of Francis of Assisi, a contemporary with whom Judah has been compared,[30] is copiously commented upon by medieval writers, Judah's life remains a mystery and virtually unknown. In spite of the fact that we have *Sefer Hasidim* before us, there is still much we should like to know in detail about the man. Even if we presume to attribute authorship to him, which is no small matter, other information about his personal life, and his opinions on important matters are still not available to us.

SEFER HASIDIM

Concerning the authorship of the book there is no complete agreement among scholars except on one point, namely, that the book is not the work of one writer but a composite of many writers.[31] This is proved by an internal examination which discloses frequent conflicting statements and sentiments. Some believe[32] that the book in its present form consists of three revisions of a text of which Judah is the original author.[33]

Moritz Gudemann is of the opinion that the task of assembling the material of *Sefer Hasidim* fell to the first and second generation of students and disciples of Judah the Pious, who had at their disposal their master's original. The place of composition, Gudemann feels, as do almost all other scholars, is in the Rhineland. S. A. Wertheimer agrees that the book is not the work of Judah the Pious alone. He is of the opinion that Judah's student Eleazar Rokeah played a major role in collating the material and adding his own to it. The text then passed into the hands of students who continued to add and arrange the material in diverse ways.[34] Abraham Epstein attributes authorship of the basic and earliest text to Samuel the Pious, Judah's father, which Judah and his student Eleazar Rokeah embellished.[35] There have been other writers who have attributed the book to other contemporaries of Judah the Pious, but such views have not been seriously received.[36]

Perhaps the most balanced and measured opinion on the question of authorship has been put forward by Fritz Baer in a view which is shared by most scholars. He says[37] that the teachings of *Sefer Hasidim* form a definite and consistent whole emanating from a specific school and reflecting the spirit of a dominating central figure, Rabbi Judah the Pious. The book itself may be regarded as a collection of ethical and religious precepts for the life of the community and the individual in Germany during the early thirteenth century. It is not an anonymous creation of successive generations; on the contrary, two or three generations of development are seen here, starting with a small group of scholars gathering themselves around a specific leading personality. This one dynamic personality sets the foundation for the *Torath Hasidim,* "Doctrine of the Hasidim," and for most of its conclusions. Baer feels that the tradition ascribing the book to Judah the Pious is quite correct in the sense that Judah stands in the center of the movement. The impact of his personality on his contemporaries may be considered from many points of view. There is hardly a category of thought or action which does not receive his comment. Perhaps it would be incorrect to ascribe all views found in the book to the man directly. But it would be fair to say, in the light of previous remarks, that they come as a consequence of the real and dominating position Judah the Pious enjoyed within the movement. Perhaps in view of the many difficulties that emerge when attempting to ascribe authorship to individuals, it would be more appropriate to refer authorship to a school of thought led by Judah the Pious. This sort of ascription, group or corporate, would of necessity imply in a single work the presence of diverse and often contradictory views. And such is the case here.[38] Nevertheless, contradictions notwithstanding, the book aspires to a higher unity, which is in essence the groundwork and message of the *Haside Ashkenaz.* It represents their interpretation of "Pietism." Naturally, such interpretation embraces a good deal: their view of the reality around them, their interpretation of ritual observance, their conception of Jewishness, of the relationship of man to God, of sin, prayer, and whatever may fall under the rubric of theology and spirituality. Observations on magic, death, and immortality and comments on miscellaneous other subjects are also present in the work. It is this latitude in subject matter, together with the unadorned treatment, that gives the book its intrinsic value as a primary source for the movement which it represents and adorns.

The fact that it represents a departure from certain traditional rabbinic norms and categories of value accounts in part for the ambivalences and contradictions that frequently occur. The departure for new climes of opinion and feeling that characterize it, very often brings a reaction in the form of nostalgia for the older and more familiar traditional touchstones. Moreover, tradition itself, pervasive and all-penetrating as it is, very often makes us heirs of contrary and irreconcilable beliefs and views. The alternation between the old and new may therefore be viewed as being in fact less a matter of contradiction than of tension between two views for greater loyalty. Very often when deeper and more intensive probing occurs, we find that the yield of both views is complete agreement on a more sublime level of aspiration and intent. It is here that a convergence and unity involving religiosity and godliness is ultimately achieved.

In an article dealing with Jewish liturgy and its development, Dr. Judah Rosenthal brings to our attention the infusion into German Hasidism of a mystical element from former generations.[39] He traces the chain of continuity from Baghdad to Italy to the Rhineland, ultimately into the possession of Judah the Pious.

The Kolonymides, outstanding and preeminent in scholarship, served in fact as the preservers of this tradition, handing down the legacy of mysticism from father to son. Dr. Rosenthal makes further mention of the important influence that this mystical tradition exerted over the content of Jewish prayer composed by German pietists during this period. He further indicates the important influence that the pietists and the movement as a whole exerted on the entire Jewish community at that time, most especially through the "Rokeah."

With these observations in mind, certain deductions become quite apparent. The mystical tradition, complex and devious as it is, possesses a higher unity which makes blood brothers of diverse elements and points of view. Once again, the lack of absolute unity and agreement on all religious dicta gives an added dimension of historicity to this movement which in fact did not resolve all of its own problems systematically. Our book leaves us, so to speak, in *medias res* not at the end of a movement but in its middle, which happens to be the most advanced stage that German pietism achieved.

THE PIOUS

In defining the nature of "piety" and the "pious" we can do so from two points of view. One view is that of the masses as reflected in contemporary literature. The other, perhaps more important and to which we will restrict ourselves, is the definition garnered from the book itself.[40] Here, broadly speaking, although a case could be made for additional and, if hard pressed, infinite subtleties and nuances, three main categories of behavior and attitude single out "the pious"; serenity of mind, altruism, and an ascetic renunciation of the things of this world.[41]

A more detailed enumeration of the component elements comprising these major rubrics would be as follows: indifference to offenses of all sorts,[42] doing deeds of kindness,[43] controlling the evil inclination in all its varied manifestations,[44] avoiding all idle and useless occupations and pastimes,[45] purity of intent and the doing of everything almost to extreme for the "sake of heaven."[46] Baer is quite right in saying[47] that all these manifestations of pietism were elicited by a demand embodied in a higher form of law, *Ius Divinum,* heavenly law. The pietist must at times veer from *Ius Positivum,* the demands of conventional law of halakha, in order to fulfill the dictates of "heavenly law."[48]

We find *Sefer Hasidim* describing the substance of pietism as the duty to act beyond the limit of the law.[49] That the law does not represent the ideal optimum of justice has its genesis in Talmudic literature.[50] We have statements in *Sefer Hasidim* to the effect that there may be things which the Torah permits and yet if a man practices them he will be brought to judgment because of them, for man must realize that the Torah permits them only because of the evil inclination.[51] Baer identifies this "heavenly law" which involves human relationships with natural human fairness and equity. Concerning relations between God and man this would provide a stricter interpretation and application of ritual and religious practices. This new line of action governed by good heart and conscience would naturally well up from the soul's assimilation of the divine spirit.

It is quite reasonable to assert that the distinctive element in "pietism" which gives it its most prominent characteristic is the striving to fulfill heavenly law, a demand which is additional, self-imposed by conscience and good heart, a law which is beyond the immediate claims of the traditional law or halakha.

PIETISM AND ASCETICISM

The ascetic strain found within the pietism of the *Haside Ashkenaz* is touched upon by numerous authors. To my mind the subject has not really been given its proper perspective. Baer tries to show differences that exist between the ascetic proclivities of the *Haside Ashkenaz* and that of non-Jewish asceticism. More, perhaps, should have been said about the similarities which are equally interesting but have received sparse comment. Dom Ursmer Berliere's remark concerning Christian mystics can very well apply to our own *Haside Ashkenaz;* that in every mystic there is an ascetic and that asceticism is at the very source of mysticism.[52] This, of course, helps to explain some of the severe forms of penance and self-denial in *Sefer Hasidim.* Moreover, we find in *Sefer Hasidim* overtones and allusions to that triple mystical root which has been sketched for the Christian mystic, purgation, illumination, and union. This is not native to Christianity alone, but was then and is today, shared by many other religions. This can be accounted for by the simple fact that so many faiths drink from a common ideational source.[53]

The period with which we are dealing and which witnesses similar mystical activity in Jewish and non-Jewish camps can be attributed to a religious influence and atmosphere, then prevalent, which affected both equally.[54]

Baer's observation is quite true that the Jewish mystic-ascetic never goes beyond a certain point in self-denial because of legal prohibitions. However, this does not set him apart from the non-Jewish mystic-ascetic in their common striving and spiritual personality. In a manner of speaking, both Christian and Jewish mystics strive and achieve the extreme within their respective faiths that is permissible. It is only in comparison with each other that this "extreme" for the Jewish mystic appears foreshortened. The Jewish mystic goes to the extremity permitted by law as does the Christian; in the latter's case, however, the extent of self-denial permitted is far more generous. The foregoing observation does not indicate at all that the basic concept and mood of Christian and Jewish mystics differ. It is the law which directs and defines the mystical ascetic personality. The Jewish mystic might well be placed beside the Christian and made to appear similar in terms of a common mood, view and aspiration. It is the rule of law and tradition which sets them apart sending them into different areas of mystical preoccupation. In this respect Baer is quite right when he says that *Haside Ashkenaz* did not and could not avoid involvement in the social scene and communal enterprise. The Christian mystical tradition with its greater latitude for escape and isolation could hold out to its contemplative mystics complete insulation from social contact and exposure. The "activists" however might well correspond in terms of their mobility and social exposure to a counterpart in Judaism, namely, the *Haside Ashkenaz.*

There are many Christian mystics who espouse in their writings, if not in their personal conduct, the virtues of the "mixed life," a balance between contemplation and action, social responsibility and mystical experience, such as is found among Jewish pietists.[55] Men like Jan Rysbroeck,[56] Nicholas of Cusa, Meister Eckhart,[57] Bernard of Clairvaux, let alone St. Francis and a host of others of lesser standing immediately come to mind.[58] One could assent in behalf of the *Haside Ashkenaz* with Ray C. Petry's observation that the call to renunciation echoes throughout the centuries of contemplation.[59] We might add in conclusion that Gershom Scholem and Baer have in their own way, made this very same observation.[60]

THE TEXTS

In addition to the problem of authorship, there is the question which of the two editions of *Sefer Hasidim* is earlier. We have today two different versions of *Sefer Hasidim:* one based on the Bologna Edition,[61] most recently republished by the Mosad Harav Kook[62] in Israel. The other version is based on the Parma MS which was prepared and edited by Jehuda Wistinetzki and Jacob Freimann.[63]

In his introduction to *Sefer Hasidim,*[64] Freimann states that he believes the Parma MS to be the older. In support of his view he points out that the Parma MS lacks the unity, systemization, and relative freedom from corrupt and variant readings already in evidence in the Bologna edition.

For immediate purposes, without entering into a critical analysis of Freimann's views, it suffices for us to agree with Freimann's observations although not necessarily with his conclusions. The Bologna edition does possess the qualities which Freimann enumerates. It does indeed possess the inner unity, style and integration which the Parma MS lacks.[65]

These considerations together with another very important fact, were decisive in the choice of the Bologna edition for our immediate use. The other important fact alluded to is this: only in the Bologna edition does the "Book of Reverence" *(Sefer Ha-Yirah)* form a complete unit in character and length to make it suitable for comprehensive treatment and translation.[66]

As matters stand at present, weighty and cogent arguments can be advanced in support of either text as representing earlier authorship. Serious criticisms, as well, can be directed against each set of arguments. When we consider both positions in this light one conclusion remains, namely, that neither view dare be dogmatic or absolute in its assertions.

THE TRANSLATION

With some exceptions the simplified method of transliteration and spelling adopted by the Jewish Publication Society has been followed, partly to facilitate reference to other matters not fully discussed here and partly because it is most helpful to English readers.

In all instances where Biblical names of persons and places and quotations occur, they are cited as found in The Jewish Publication Society version of The Bible. If there is a variant it is indicated in the notes.[67] Where transliteration of Hebrew terms has been necessary simplicity has been preferred, even, in a few instances, at the expense of consistency.[68]

The translation aims at being as literal as English idiom will permit. Words and passages not represented in the text are enclosed in parentheses or found in the notes.

For the most part, the notes contain citations from rabbinical authorities, legalistic and literary materials, which serve as sources for many of the statements found in *Sefer Hasidim*.[69]

In numerous cases, the citation only indicates where a discussion of the matter can be located or where a corroborative view is expressed. Often the source cited is from a period beyond that of Judah the Pious.

Where there are differences of opinion among standard commentators attention is drawn to this in the notes, although such differences are infrequent and seldom affect major issues.

Important variant readings and explanations that are helpful for understanding technical and recurrent terms appearing in the text can be found in the notes.

MEDIEVAL JEWISH MYSTICISM

BOOK OF THE PIOUS

BOOK OF THE PIOUS

1. This is called "Book of the Pious." Its contents are sweet and most desirable. It is written for those who fear God and revere His name. There is a Hasid whose heart desires the love of His Creator, to do His will completely. But he does not know which matters to assume, which matters to avoid, or how to immerse himself thoroughly to do his Creator's will. The reason is that hearts have become deficient. There is a Hasid who undertakes a great deal and there is one who does little, but if he knew and understood matters of piety he would do a great deal more than those who do much. It is for this reason that the "Book of the Pious" was written, so that all who fear God and those returning to their Creator with a sincere heart may see, know and understand all that they must do and all that they must avoid. This book was not written for the wicked, for if they read it much of its contents would strike them as nonsense. And if communicated to them, they would ridicule it. Concerning them Solomon in his wisdom said, "Speak not in the ear of a fool; for he will despise the wisdom of thy words" (Prov. 23:8). Similarly when Solomon wrote Proverbs, it was not intended for the wicked for even if he were to confront them with all his wisdom, it would not have availed either to better their hearts or to encourage their return (to God). He spoke only to the righteous who long for God's word; he spoke to them that they might see, understand and become wise, as it is written, "For the ways of the Lord are right, and the just do walk in them; but transgressors do stumble therein" (Hos. 14:10). This demonstrates that the path of piety, humility and fear of the Lord is a snare unto the wicked but an ascent for the righteous.

2. The author of this book who dealt with piety, humility and fear of the Lord in separate treatises, said, "I perceived for myself, and from my teachers I received understanding and instruction. It is proper for all those that fear the Lord to teach their children, students and all Israel how they can succeed in doing the will of our Creator, may His name be blessed and His fame be exalted."

His style is that of the allegory, comparing the Lord to the ways of mortals in order to reach the hearts of humans, to speak to them in their accustomed manner of hearing, to open the eyes of the blind and to enlighten uncircumcized hearts. And this is recorded in the Bible, "And His voice was like the sound of many waters" (Ezek. 43:2); "The Lord shall roar like a lion" (Hos. 11:10). He also likens His image to that of His creatures: "His eyes are like doves" (Cant. 5:12); and there are many other such examples: "His legs are as pillars of marble" (Cant. 5:15). All this is done in order to address them in their accustomed manner of hearing.

3. "The memory of the righteous shall be for a blessing" (Prov. 10:7), i.e., the memory of the Righteous One of the world will be for a blessing.[1] Each time we invoke the revered and awesome name of God we are enjoined to bless Him in the sacred tongue, may His name be blessed.[2] Even those of lesser knowledge will understand that this is comparable to a man whose son or loved one has gone on some distant journey; when he refers to him he does so saying, "My son, may he be remembered in peace this day, may all go well with him." And whereas we say of the deceased, "His repose be peace,"[3] all the more so are we enjoined (to say) concerning the Holy One, blessed be He, who is living and enduring, "may the revered name of our Creator be blessed." Concerning this it was said, "He who hears his neighbor invoke God's name (in vain) should excommunicate him, and if he fails to do so he is himself excommunicated."[4]

4. It is reported of a certain pious man that while seated in a wedding hall he heard one of the singers at the dance employing God's name in his song. The pious man excommunicated him for each single offense. Even demons do not invoke God's name in vain, as it is stated in the tractate Megillah, "Perhaps it was a demon? but we do know by way of tradition, they do not invoke the name of God in vain."[1]

5. "Thou shalt surely rebuke they neighbor" (Lev. 19:17). We are commanded to rebuke any Israelite who is resigned and careless of even one of the 248 positive commandments, or if he has violated one of the negative commands. And the sages tell us that he who has an opportunity to rebuke any Israelite concerning a positive or negative command and fails to do so is punished for all

4

(the transgressions).¹ As we have studied (Talmud), "He who has the opportunity to rebuke and protest the actions of his household members and fails to do so is punished because of them. If it involves people of his city he is held responsible because of them, if it involves the entire world he is held responsible for the entire world."² Whence do we know that we must return a second time to reprove someone if he has failed to respond at first? It is stated, "Whence do we deduce (the command) that if one has rebuked a first time he must rebuke his neighbor once again." It is stated, "Thou shalt surely rebuke."³ He must do so in a manner commensurate with the qualities of the one who is being rebuked; if he be kindly let him reprove him benignly, if he be difficult let him rebuke him accordingly. Let him speak to him in parables and give proofs to enable him to restore his mind to his will. And he shall not favor an elder or superior if he wishes to avoid punishment because of (either of) them. He should warn them of their wicked deeds with impartiality, even when involving a teacher.⁴ For thus said the wise man, "Where there is a profanation of God's name, one does not grant respect even to a teacher."⁵ And they (the rabbis) said further, "Rebuke"; this implies a teacher towards his student. How do we know that a student may do similarly to his teacher? Read the text: "Thou shalt surely rebuke, in all cases."⁶ We are obliged to rebuke transgressors and to shame them with their sins to the extent that they strike, insult and curse us. He who rebukes is obliged to reprove (purge) himself for that transgression and to rectify his (own) way before rebuking his neighbor. For if he fails to do so his neighbor will not accept his reproofs. Thus did they say, "Gather yourselves together, yea, gather together," first adorn (correct) thyself and then adorn (correct) others.⁷ And let no man rest without exploring all means to cause his neighbor to walk the straight path, furthering him from (assisting him against) transgression in worldly and spiritual matters. He who restrains himself from rebuking is guilty of his neighbor's punishment; for it is written, "Thou shalt not bear sin because of him"⁸ (Lev. 19:17). And if he has rebuked him and his neighbor has not responded the rebuker is exempt from punishment for the sin. The rebuker nevertheless receives merit because he has admonished him to walk the straight path and to shun wrong, as it is explained in the paragraph,

"Therefore, O thou son of man, etc. . . ." (Ezek. 23:9) "Nevertheless if thou warn the wicked of his way to turn from it and he turn not from his way he shall die in his iniquity, but thou hast delivered thy soul" (Ezek. 23:9). The root of this commandment "and not bear sin because of him" (Lev. 19:17), is that a man should not reprove his fellowman with anger or embarrassment,[9] but first quietly and privately that he not become insolent and recalcitrant and add wrong to his transgression.[10] Thus did they say, "I might conclude that he may rebuke him even if his neighbor suffers embarrassment"; read the text, "Thou shalt not bear sin because of him" (Lev. 19:17).[11]

6. "Thou shalt not bear false witness against thy neighbor" (Exod. 20:13). By implication of this negative command it is forbidden to say a shameful thing about a neighbor not in his presence, i.e., that if he were to hear it, it would anger him.[1] As it is written, "Thou sittest and speakest against thy brother, thou slanderest thine own mother's son" (Ps. 50:20).

But if he has committed sins and has been reproved privately but he has not accepted (the reproofs) then it is permissible to reprimand him publicly for his evil doings, with or without his presence.[2]

7. Of what manner is the root of piety? When a man's heart inclines toward qualities of piety and it is made difficult for him because all mock him and shame him and say things to torment him and recall his former evil deeds, let him not leave his piety because of the scorners, but let him acquire good qualities little by little, day after day: "he that gathereth little by little shall increase" (Prov. 13:11). Concerning this it is stated, "If thou art wise, thou art wise for thyself" (Prov. 9:12). Concerning the scorners it is written "They make a man an offender by words" (Isa. 29:21), i.e., they (the scorners) speak badly about those who perform the commandments. It is a great sin to say to a penitent, "Remember thy former deeds"[1] after he has evidenced through good deeds his desire to acquire the qualities of piety. He is not disturbed by the laughter of the scorners. Those that recall his former deeds are regarded as if closing the door to the penitent. And let him say to himself that his being shamed will be counted for him as a great merit and as righteousness.[2] And the pure fear of God enters his heart and purifies his heart and body of all evil because he will be aided from heaven to be strengthened in the

fear of God. And so they said, "He who comes to be purified is assisted from heaven."[3] And they prepare for him to make full repentance, for the doors of repentance are not shut.[4] And precept leads to precept,[5] and now as the man enters through the doors of repentance he will pray day and night before his Creator that He rescue him from Divine Justice and there occur no stumbling through himself. And to the extent that a man treads in his piety and has no inclination to turn aside from his meritorious way—for it is upright in his sight—so the Master of Uprightness will lead him in the upright path. And thus David said, "Good and upright is the Lord; therefore doth He instruct sinners in the way. He guideth the humble in justice; and He teacheth the humble His way" (Ps. 25:8). And as he enters piety with difficulty so will it be the more difficult for him to leave his good way because of shame, because people might say, thus is it now known that this man strives for outward appearances only[6] and in order to deceive people he has feigned piety, and it is forbidden to deceive people, even a gentile.[7] And because piety is difficult to achieve initially it is good to start during youth, as it is written, "Remember then thy Creator in the days of thy youth" (Eccl. 12:1); "and even when he is old he will not depart from it" (Prov. 22:6). For the repentance of an old man, when he is aged and the desires are gone, resembles a man indulging in slander with his tongue gone and he speaks no more. But when a man returns while yet in his strength and might and his passion threatens to make itself master over him and he subdues it, this sort of repentance is the most praiseworthy. And a mighty act he performs indeed through controlling his intense and strong passion. Concerning this it is said, "and he that ruleth his spirit (rather) than he that taketh a city" (Prov. 16:32). And for each matter which is difficult for the individual but which he nevertheless accomplishes, his reward is very great.[8]

8. When Rabbi Simeon ben Gamaliel and Rabbi Ishmael went forth to be killed, said Rabbi Simeon b. Gamaliel to Rabbi Ishmael "I do not know why I am going forth to be killed." He said, "Perhaps when you were expounding in public, your heart rejoiced and your heart was gratified." He said, "You have consoled me."[1] And so should every man do, he should repent of his evil doings without ostentation and let him go and perform his tasks and matters privately,

let his heart not profit at all from his good works; also all matters relative to piety let him do in concealment. For it is already stated, "conceal thy things" (Prov. 25:2) "and walk humbly with thy God" (Mic. 6:8). And let a man not claim credit for himself that his intentions are heavenly. Let him beware lest his heart profit or rejoice. For if his heart rejoices before the world, he has indeed already received a part of the reward for that command in this world. If his heart rejoiced against his will, that is to say without his knowledge or intent, let him condition his heart to overcome his passion and let him desist from that act in which his heart rejoiced. For many of those now deceased performed this specific deed and performed meritorious acts without number; they have passed on to their eternal rest and the matter is forgotten, they have left no remembrance because their memory is forgotten in this world with none to recall them, but their memory is for the after-life. Therefore what advantage or profit is mine if they praise me in this world? So should he think at all times also at night when retiring. He must be concerned lest eternal sleep overtake him and he will awaken no more. Wherefore should he continue to rejoice that they praise him in this world? All is vanity and a striving after wind.

9. The main strength of piety from beginning to end is that although they scoff at him he does not forsake his piety, his intent is for heaven's sake and he does not look at the countenances of women: especially so among other men where women are customarily seen, for example, if he has been in the wedding hall where the women were garbed in choicest ornaments and all were gazing but he did not stare, for that will he merit the great good that is laid up, as it is written, "which thou hast laid up for those that fear thee" (Ps. 31:20). And his eye will be satiated with the Divine Glory: "Thine eyes shall see the king in his beauty" (Isa. 33:17). For this reason it is best for the individual when he meets a woman, whether single or married, whether a gentile woman or Jewish, whether she be of age or a minor, to turn his face aside from looking at her. Thus do we find in Job (31:1), "I made a covenant with mine eyes; how then should I look upon a maid." And thus is it written in the book of Ben Sira, "Avert your eyes from a beautiful woman, lest you stumble and incur penalties for her." [1] (So Isa. 33:15) "And shutteth his eyes

8

from looking upon evil" refers to him who gazes not upon women at the time when they stand by their wash.[2] When they wash their garments and lift their skirts so as not to soil them, they uncover their legs, and we know a woman's leg is a sexual incitement[3] and so said the sage, "nothing interposes better before desire, than closing one's eyes."[4]

10. The essence of piety is to apply oneself constantly to things, where his passions are most challenging, such as evil gossip, the evil inclination, vanities, not to speak falsely, not to stare at women or speak of worldly curiosities or walk about idly; implicit in all this is evil passion. Thus he should not swear at all, nor invoke God's name in vain, and so in all similar matters that go on constantly, where his passion overpowers him and he cannot withstand (he will be able to resist) only if he has been trained from childhood. Therefore let a man train his children in these matters while they are yet small and when they grow old they will not forsake them or set them aside; as it is written, "And even when he is old he will not depart from it" (Prov. 22:6). Take, for example, tallith and phylacteries, many men of quality wish to garb themselves with fringes and put on the phylacteries but refrain from doing so because of embarrassment; however all matters in which a man is trained (to do so) in childhood, when he grows up and attempts to forsake (them) it will be as difficult for him as death. But if a man strengthens himself in Torah and commandments and good deeds, then it becomes difficult for him to depart from them because of the embarrassment; people will say all that he has done so far has been to deceive people, as has been mentioned. He is called *hasid,* which is derived from *hasadim* (kindness).[1] He is also called *hasid* because of the term *hasidah* (stork) (Deut. 14:18) which Onkelos translates *huraitha* (white bird). And it is written, "not now shall he be ashamed, neither shall his face now wax pale" (Isa. 29:22), which has the meaning of insult and shame that if they insult him and cause his face to become white and he like one deaf can not hear and like a mute does not open his mouth and does not insult anyone, then he is called pious.[2] And in the hereafter his face will shine brightly and he will succeed to sit in the seven classes of righteous men who will receive the Shekhina and enjoy the Divine Glory.[3] As it is written, "Arise, shine for thy light is

come and the glory of the Lord is risen upon thee etc. . . . But upon thee the Lord will arise and His glory shall be seen upon thee. And nations shall walk by thy light and kings by the brightness of thy rising" (Isa. 60:1-3). These seven classes enjoy Divine Glory.

11. One is not considered pious unless he is able to overlook personal grievances. If people come before him who have wronged him and have dealt with him unworthily, and now are sorry and seek his forgiveness; that which is in their power to correct of the wrong which they caused, they correct, and for that which they cannot remedy, they repent and seek his pardon, and agree to accept any judgement he sees fit to pass upon them. And when this one sees that it is in his power to do evil to them and repay them in kind, he forgives them with a whole heart and does not do evil to them. Because of this he is called pious, as it is written, "Return thou backsliding Israel, Saith the Lord; I will not frown upon you for I am merciful" (Jer. 3:12). And so the children of Jacob, when they sinned against Joseph, he forgave and did not repay in kind. And this is the root of *Hasiduth,* he must do beyond the line of strict justice in all matters, as it is written "and gracious in all his works" (Ps. 145:17).

12. The root of *Hasiduth* is fear of the Lord. If a man desires some matter of enjoyment and turns aside from his passion only because of fear of God and not because he fears retributions in the world to come, nor because of the enjoyment of this world and the world to come, but he rather fears that he will not be perfect in the love of the Creator, may His name be blessed, as it is written, "Thou shalt be wholehearted with the Lord thy God" (Deut. 18:13); this person is called a God-fearing man. The great and singular restraint is forsaking foods, for saturation with foods brings evil imaginations. How so? If there be before him a meal of fish or meat or of other dainties let him not resist from eating at all but for the fear of God let him not fill his stomach to the full reach of his appetite.[1] It is the same with respect to one to whom a meritorious deed presents itself and it is difficult for him to do it, and (nevertheless) he does not desist from acting. And so we find with Abraham, "for now I know that thou art a God-fearing man" (Gen. 22:12).

13. The foundation of the fear of God is the trial. For the essence of fear becomes apparent in the time of trial. And as fear is apparent

when involving passion for women, so is it recognizable in all sorts of passion. And the Holy One, blessed be He, does not put man to a trial except when He intends to do good to him; Satan, who embodies the attribute of strict justice, comes before God and says, "Lord of the Universe, it would not be proper to do good to him until he proves himself in trial." Therefore the just are sworn to conquer their passion.[1] And thus when He brought good to Saul and his children He tried him, and so with Abraham and Job.[2] Man should always be deliberate in the fear of the Lord,[3] answering softly, turning back anger,[4] speaking peacefully with his brothers and close ones, even with a gentile in the street, in order that he be beloved above and favored below and acceptable to human beings. They said concerning Rabbi Yohanan ben Zakkai, a man never was first in saluting him not even a gentile.[5] And let a man be deliberate in fear of the Lord and understanding to think subtle thoughts for the improvement of the world and the honor of heaven. In the end the words of every man who is God-fearing are heard. As it is stated, "The end of the matter, all having been heard: fear God" (Eccl. 12:13).[6] A man who possesses learning but is devoid of works is analogous to one to whom have been given the inner keys but not the outer ones by which he shall enter; and how shall he enter?[7]

14. The root of loving God is loving God with all your heart (Deut. 6:4). Our Creator commanded us to serve him with love,[1] that the love of our soul be bound up with His soul in joy and in His love and with a good heart. And the joy of this love is of such intensity and so overpowers the heart of those who love God, that even after many days of not being with his wife and having a great desire for her, in the hour that a man ejaculates he does not find it as satisfying as the intensity and power of loving[2] God and finding joy in his Creator. And all the pleasures of playing with his children are as naught compared to the pleasures of the heart of the man who loves God with all his heart and soul and with all his might, i.e., with all his thoughts, about how to love God and how to make the public acquire merit and sanctify God's name, and how to devote himself with love to the Creator,[3] as did Phineas the priest who dedicated himself with love for his Creator to be zealous in His name.

11

Let him not covet money in a situation where there is a Sanctification of God's name if he resists taking money, as we find with Abraham, "that I will not take a thread or a shoe latchet" (Gen. 14:23). And so (it was) with Elisha who did not want to take money from Naaman. Let him not neglect the study of the Law because of pleasures, playing with his children or attachment to his wives. Also let him give up leisurely walks, meeting with women, sweet songs, in order that his heart may be whole in the joy of God, toiling and laboring in that which is the will of the Creator. He should take a lesson from one of flesh and blood. If he knew a matter to be the desire of a king, he would not yield nor rest until he fulfilled the will of the king, who is a worm like himself. He would be overjoyed that his deeds received the notice of the king and especially if it met with the will of the Creator who is eternal. Therefore must he labor all the more and seek how to fulfill the will of His commandments. He who serves out of love, occupies himself with Torah and commandments, goes in paths of proper wisdom and occupies himself with Torah and loves God with great love, not for any other reason, and not for fear of evil, nor for the purpose of inheriting the good. But he serves in truth, because the Holy One, blessed be He, is truth and in the end the good will come because of it.[4] He must love the Creator with a great and strong love until he becomes sick because of his love, as the man who is love-sick for the affections of a woman and reels constantly because of his love, when he sits, rises, goes and comes, also when he eats and drinks. He neither sleeps nor slumbers because of this love. Greater than this should love of the Creator be in the hearts of those who love Him and they should be absorbed in it constantly,[5] as we were commanded, "with all thy heart, with all thy soul . . ." (Deut. 6:4); and this is what Solomon in his wisdom said by the way of simile: "For I am love-sick" (Cant. 2:5). And this is a matter as clear as day and sun, for all who know that love of the Creator is not bound up with the heart of man until he is absorbed in it continuously, so as, for example, to forsake all else in the world outside of Him, as He commanded us "with all thy heart" (Deut. 6:4). This is impossible except through the apprehension of the mind. Therefore this is the truth, and the sum of it all is, that man must understand and study in the wisdoms and disciplines that make known to him his Master [6] according to the intellectual ability that he possesses to understand, consider and comprehend. [7] And the Creator, blessed be His name and exalted be His revered and awesome fame, commanded us to love and fear His name, as it is written "and thou shalt love the Lord thy God" (Deut. 6:4); and it is said, "thou shalt fear the Lord thy God" (Deut. 6:13). And which is the way in which to love Him and fear Him? In the hour that the individual comprehends the great and wondrous works of God, the Holy One, blessed be He, which are beyond assessment and limit, he immediately loves, praises, glorifies and yearns deeply to know that great, revered and awesome name. [8] And thus did David say, "My soul thirsteth for God for the living God" (Ps. 42:3). And when he reflects upon these matters he will be startled, he will fear, and will tremble that he is a very small and lowly creature standing with poor and scanty knowledge before Him. [9] And so did David say, "When I behold Thy heavens the work of Thy fingers etc. . . . . What is man that Thou art mindful of him" (Ps. 8:4).

15. Concerning the root of humility, one must remove oneself from a situation involving high office and honor, and let him not include himself with other individuals. How so? If he was before his teacher and he remembered a question or some query that he posed or some answer that he supplied, let him not say to his teacher or his friend, "So have I answered, so have I asked," but "So have you asked," in order that his heart may not be gratified. [1] Also let him give his teacher or friend the honor and not himself. For such do we find with Moses, when he said to Joshua, "Choose us our men" (Exod. 17:9). [2] From this Rabbi Gamaliel derived and wrote, "The matter pleases me and my colleagues." [3] And it is also written that the Holy One, blessed be He, said to Isaiah, "Whom shall I send, and who will go for us?" (Isa. 6:8). From this the Torah indicated the path of humility for scholars. If you question why it is written, "Whom shall I send," and it is not written "Shall we send," the answer is: let it not be said that there are two powers governing the universe. [4] And he should mention his friend's name before his own in all matters, in French, "vous et moi," and let him not say "moi et vous." Thus the Schools of Hillel and Shammai were wont to do. In relating

the opinions of both each one mentioned the other's reason before indicating its own,[5] even in worldly matters.[6] And when he sits in council and knows both question and a good answer, let him not jump to speak until he sees that it will not occur to others, then may he speak.[7] And when he hears his friend speaking of a certain matter and he knows of it, likewise let him not leap and interrupt his friend's remarks, saying, "I know about it"; rather let him be silent and hear him out.[8] For there will be many instances wherein he will hear explanations that he did not hear previously. Moreover what profit is there to glory in the matter saying, "I know as well as you do." The end of the matter is that in every way that one is able to diminish his own honor in order to magnify the honor of those that fear God let him do so, as it is written, "In whose eyes a vile person is despised, but he honoreth them that fear the Lord" (Ps. 15:4). And if he sees that others pride themselves through humility resulting in his own embarrassment, let him listen to them. For example, if they are greater than he is and they do not wish to walk before him, i.e., they say, "We are also humble," and because of this he is embarrassed in that he must walk before them; he is exposed to embarrassment because they urge him to walk in front and he grieves lest they say of him, "How impudent this one is who goes before us, it is we who are greater than he, and see how he magnifies himself because of it," and in this they pride themselves. In spite of this he should bear the embarrassment in order to respect them, and it will be regarded as a sin and transgression on their part in that they honor themselves at the expense of his embarrassment. Let him not honor his friend in a way that causes him embarrassment. For example, he (his friend) is customarily called by name, but he calls him "teacher," and he (his friend) is embarrassed by this, in that he feels mocked and ridiculed.[9] (When studying with two teachers) Let him not praise one in the presence of the other[10] nor praise his teacher's teacher in his teacher's presence, that he should say to his teacher, "So and so your teacher,[11] etc. . . . ." Here is a case where students spoke to their teacher Rabbi Eliezer concerning Rabbi Eliezer's teacher Rabbi Yochanan Ben Zakkai, saying, "Your colleagues have already been polled concerning you and have permitted it."[12] Although a person should not profit from his humility,[13] as has already been stated; one should not extoll his own

14

humility since it is written, "Let another man praise thee and not thine own mouth" (Prov. 27:2), however if he wishes to praise himself to his students and friends in order that they learn from his ways, he may praise himself, as David stated, "And I was single-hearted with Him" (Ps. 18:22), "For I have kept the ways of the Lord." And so do we find a scholar who related to his students his good deeds for which he achieved longevity.[14] Let a man not stand in a place where he is being praised,[15] for it is impossible that he should not profit thereof. All the good deeds that a man might perform, are as a dish without salt if he be lacking in humility.[16] And all humility which has not in it fear of heaven is as victuals without seasoning. This world compares to the world to come as sleeping to wakefulness. In a dream one is not ashamed. For if one were ashamed, imaginings such as, for example, that he is sleeping with a woman and playing with her would not occur to him. He would not do things (in his dream) that he would be ashamed of if they were done while awake. The reason is that dreams come as a result of imaginings.[17] If a man entertains impure thoughts he is not ashamed of them (his impure fancies), because (he realizes) that a man does not know or have an understanding of what his neighbor imagines in his heart, (for this reason) therefore he is not embarrassed during his dream. He who is God-fearing with all his heart and because of fear of his Creator does not imagine evil things when awake, will also never be visited with evil imaginings in his dreams.[18] And so did Ezekiel (4:14) say, "My soul hath not been polluted." I did not imagine by day and therefore did not come to pollution at night.[19] And so did our rabbis explain, "Thou shalt keep thee from every evil thing" (Deut. 23:10). A man should not imagine by day and come to pollution by night.[20]

16. A man should not look at a woman even though she be unattractive,[1] neither at the colored garments of a woman, neither at animals during mating,[2] even though he be "full of eyes" as the Angel of Death. The rabbis have taught, "Thou shalt keep thee from every evil thing" (Deut. 23:10). From this Rabbi Phineas ben Jair makes the following[3] deduction: "Torah leads to zeal, and zeal leads to care, and care leads to cleanliness, and cleanliness leads to self-control, and self-control leads to purity, and purity leads to fear of sin, and fear of sin leads to saintliness, and saintliness leads to the

resurrection of the dead; and saintliness is greater than all, as it is written, "Then Thou spokest in vision to Thy godly ones" (Ps. 89:20). Others say humility is greater than them all, as it is written, "Because the Lord hath annointed me to bring good tidings unto the humble" (Isa. 61:1). To bring good tidings to the saintly is not written, but to the humble. But the wicked who have evil imaginings and do not guard themselves against evil, come to uncleanliness at night, and to dreams, and to impure fancies leading to pollution. And as there is no shame for the dream, so is there no embarrassment for the wicked with their deeds in this world, as it is written, "Yet they are not at all ashamed, neither know they how to blush" (Jer. 6:15). And all those wicked who imagine evil things and do not dispel them with study of the Torah or with other means, in the world to come The Holy One, blessed be He, will give recompense; for in the same measure that a man commits evil so will he be repaid.[4] Even though humility brings a person to the world to come, humility does not exist in the world to come, and no person will be able to honor his neighbor by saying, "Sit beside me." For each one will rest on his couch and each one will come in peace to the place that is prepared for him. And each one who humbles himself in this world and is able to rule over himself and take a position of leadership and administration in the community, and has no desire to exalt himself, as did the Sons of Bathyra (Elders of Bathyra) who resigned their leadership in deference to Hillel who was greater than they,[5] and all others like them, will be at the forefront in the world to come.

17. Concerning the root of study, the individual must steep himself in study and know the performance of each commandment, as it is written, "A good understanding have all they that do thereafter" (Ps. 111:10). It is not written, "All they that study," but "They that do." A man should not read and study and be contumacious with his father or teacher or one who is greater than he. He rather studies on the condition that he teach, observe and do, and this is study for its own sake.[1] And whoever studies the Law not for its own sake, better for him that he were not created.[2] And anyone who is engaged in the study of the Law and knows its commandments and does not fulfill them, woe unto him and his fortune, that he toils in this world in order to acquire Gehenna.[3] And more severe is his punishment than one who

16

did not learn and did not know how to guard himself, for he understands and deliberately rebels.[4] If an individual understands, he must let his words come forth audibly, and let his ears and eyes be free of all things, and (let him) be open-eyed when studying the Law.[5] Where from do we know this? From Ezekiel, as it is written, "Son of man behold with thine eyes and hear with thine ears and set thy heart upon all that I shall show thee" (Ezek. 40:4). And is not the entire matter concluded *a minori ad majus!* If in the case of the Temple which was measured with a yardstick, God said to him to apply his heart, eyes, and ears; would it not be all the more so in the case of matters of the Law, which are as mountains hanging by a hair. One must set aside study periods for the Law each day and night to fulfill what is written: "Thou shalt meditate therein day and night"[6] (Josh. 1:8). One who studies more and one who studies less are equal so long as the heart is directed towards heaven.[7] And better is a little with fear of God, than the abundance of the wicked who study all the day and do not practice.

18. The root of prayer is joyousness of heart in the Holy One, blessed be He,[1] as it is written, "Glory ye in His holy name; let the heart of them rejoice that seek the Lord" (I Chron. 16:10). And that is why David, King of Israel, used to play on his lute all of his prayers and songs in order to fill his heart with joy in his love for God.[2] And when an individual prays he must direct his heart to Him before Whom he stands.[3] Five things prevent prayer even though its time has arrived. These are they: ritual purity of the hands, covering one's nakedness, purity of the place of prayer, matters that distract, and the intent of the heart. "Ritual purity of the hands," how so? He washes his hands with water unto the joint of the wrist, in French *jointure,* and then let him pray. If he has been walking and the time of prayer has arrived and he has no water, let him walk until (he reaches) a place of water, wash his hands and then pray. If there is between him and the water more than four miles[4] let him cleanse his hands with pebbles, or with sand, or on a post and pray, as it has been said,[5] "In what case was this said 'before him,' but 'behind him' we do not oblige him to return, but only up to a mile." But if he has gone more than a mile he then cleanses his hands with pebbles, sand or on a post. "Covering one's nakedness," how so?[6] Even

17

though he has covered his nakedness in the manner that he covers himself for the reading of the *Shema,* let him not pray until he covers his bosom. And if he has not covered his bosom because of circumstance and has nothing with which to cover himself, since he has covered his shame and prayed he has done his duty. But at the outset he should not do so. "Cleanliness of the place of prayer," how so?[7] Let him not stand in a filthy place and pray, nor in a bathhouse, nor in a privy, nor in a dung heap, nor in a place which has not a presumptive status of ritual cleanliness until investigated. The sum of the matter is that one does not pray in a place where he cannot recite the *Shema.* And in the same manner that one removes himself from excrement, similarly does one remove himself from urine and from bad odors and from indecent sights for prayer, as he would remove himself for the recitation of the *Shema.* If during the prayer one finds excrement in his place, since he has sinned by not investigating prior to praying let him repeat his prayers in a clean place. If one has been in the midst of prayer and seen excrement in front of him, if he is able to go forward putting a distance of four cubits between, let him go forth. If he is unable to do so, let him remove it to the side and if he is unable to do this, let him cease praying. "Matters that distract," how so? If one has had need to evacuate and has prayed, his prayer is an abomination. He repeats his prayers after taking care of his needs.[8] If he is able to contain himself for the time needed to traverse a parasang, his prayer is acceptable. But even so, let him not pray until he has examined himself thoroughly, let him remove phlegm, mucous, all spittle and filth of the nose, and then let him pray. One who belches, yawns or sneezes deliberately during his prayers, in French, *tousser, bâiller, éternuer,* is disgraceful. But if he has examined himself before praying and was overcome, it is of no consequence. If during his prayer he has chanced upon spittle, let him remove it with his prayer shawl or clothing, but if he be exceedingly sensitive and troubled thereby, let him cast it behind him, in order that he not be troubled during prayer. If he breaks wind during prayer unwittingly, let him be silent until the odor subsides and then return to his prayer. If he has had need to break wind and suffered greatly being unable to contain himself, let him remove himself a distance of four cubits, wait until the odor subsides, say,

"Lord of all the universes, You have created me orifices and orifices, hollows and hollows. Before the throne of Thy glory is revealed and apparent our revilement all the days of our lives and that we are worms in our death." And he prays once again in his place. If he has been in the midst of prayer and urine has dripped on his knees, he waits until it ceases and returns to the place in his prayers where he has stopped. And if he has paused for an interval of such duration as would have enabled him to conclude the prayer, let him return to the beginning. Similarly if he has urinated, he pauses for the duration of an interval necessary to walk four cubits and then prays.[9] "Directing one's heart," how so? A prayer which is devoid of inwardness let him repeat and pray with inwardness. If his mind has been confused and his heart troubled, he is forbidden to pray until his mind becomes settled. In what way is inwardness achieved? He should free his mind of all thoughts as if he were standing before the Lord. Therefore he must rest a bit before prayer[10] in order to direct the prayer inwardly, and then let him pray with prayers and supplications. And let him not regard his prayer as if he were carrying some heavy burden which he casts aside and then moves on. Therefore, he should sit down after prayer and then leave. The scholars of former years tarried one hour before prayer and one hour after prayer and prolonged their prayers one hour.[11] A person who is drunk should not pray,[12] and if he prays his prayer is an abomination, because there is no inwardness. But when he becomes sober let him recite again his prayers with inwardness. While under the influence of drink let him not pray. But if he has prayed, his prayer is acceptable. Who is regarded as being drunk? One who cannot speak before a king. But one under the influence of drink is able to speak before a king and does not blunder, but even if this be the case, if he has drunk a quarter of wine, let him not pray until the wine wears off. And so one does not rise to pray out of laughter,[13] in French *rieur,* or out of lightheadedness or scoffing, or out of conversation, or out of strife, or out of anger, only out of the study of the Law, and such law that he does not have to investigate, namely, defined laws.[14] If he has been travelling by ship, or has been in a place of danger, in a place where there are hordes of wild beasts and robbers, and the hour of prayer has arrived,[15] he recites one prayer and this is it: "The needs of Thy people Israel are great and they are impatient; may it be Thy will God, our God and God of our fathers, that You assign to each and everyone enough for his maintenance and to each individual enough for his requirements, and that which is best in Thy sight do. Blessed art Thou, O Lord, Who hears prayer." And he recites it as he goes, and if he is able to remain stationary he stands, and when he reaches a settlement and his mind is set at ease he repeats the prayer according to the institution of the Eighteen Benedictions. Of eight things must the person who prays be circumspect[16] —and do them. And if he has been pressed or overcome or if he has transgressed and has not performed them they do not hinder the matter, and these are they: standing, facing the Holy Temple, preparation of the body, modulating the voice, arranging the attire, preparation of the place, kneeling and prostration. "Standing," how so?[17] One does not pray except while standing. If he has been seated in a ship or wagon, if he is able to stand let him stand, if not, let him sit in his place and pray. One who is sick prays even though sitting, and this applies only when he is able to direct his mind. Similarly the thirsty and the hungry are classified as being ill. If it is possible for them to direct their mind, let them pray; if not, they should not pray until they eat and drink. If he has been riding on an animal, even though there is someone to hold his animal until he complete his prayer, let him not descend but rather sit in his place and pray in order that his mind be at ease. "Facing the Holy Temple," how so?[18] If he has been standing outside the Holy Land, he turns his countenance towards the land of Israel and prays. If he has been standing in the Holy Land he directs his countenance towards the Holy of Holies. A blind person or one who cannot tell directions or one travelling on a ship, let him direct his heart towards the Divine Presence and pray. "Preparation of the body," how so? If he has been in the midst of prayer he must align his feet one beside the other.[19] He casts his eyes downward and directs his heart as if looking earthward, and let his heart be turned upward as if he were standing in heaven. And let him place his hands as though bound upon his heart, the right upon the left, and stand as a slave before his master in fear

20

and trembling. Let him not place his hands upon his loins. "Adjusting one's attire," how so?[20] He adjusts his clothing at the outset, straightens himself and adorns himself, as it is written, "Worship the Lord in the beauty of holiness" (Ps. 29:2). Let him not stand in prayer with his purse, nor with a bare head, nor with exposed feet, if the custom of people of that place is not to stand before a superior except with shoes. While praying it is prohibited to take hold of a Scroll of the Law or phylacteries, because his mind is engaged. Let him not hold money or an object in his hand. But during the Festival he prays with his palm branch in his hand because that is the commandment of the day. The custom of the sages and their students was not to pray except when fully dressed.[21] "Preparation of the place," how so?[22] Let him stand in a low place and pray. Let him turn his face to the walls. He should open the windows or the doors towards Jerusalem to pray towards them, for thus do we find in the case of Daniel, "His windows were open in his upper chamber towards Jerusalem" (Dan. 6:11). He establishes a place for prayer. One does not pray in a ruin, neither behind the synagogue, only if he directs his countenance towards the synagogue. It is prohibited to sit beside one who stands in prayer or to pass before him unless he is removed from him four cubits. He should not stand in a place higher than three handbreadths or more and pray, neither on a bed, a bench or on a chair. If he has been standing in an elevated edifice and it is four cubits in length by four cubits in width, which are the dimensions of a house, it is considered a garret and it is permissible to pray. Thus if it is surrounded with a partition on all sides, even though it lacks four cubits, it is permissible to pray there. "Modulating the voice," how so?[23] He should not raise his voice in prayer, and should not pray only in his heart but articulate the words with his lips, sounding it to his ear. He should not cause his voice to be heard except if he has been sick or unable to direct his mind until it causes his voice to be heard; then it is permissible, except that he not be in public, so as not to disturb the thought of others hearing his voice. "Bending the knee," how so?[24] He who prays should bend the knee five times; with the first blessing at its beginning and end; and at *Modim* beginning and end; and when he finishes the prayer he bows and prostrates himself taking three steps backwards.[25] When he concludes the prayer, let him bow to the left which is the right of the Holy One, blessed be He, then to the right, and then lift his head from bowing. And when he bends the knee, he bends with "blessed," and when he assumes his upright position he does so with the "Name." [26] In all of these bowings he is required to bend until all the vertebrae of the spine seem to be loosened. Let him make himself as a bow, and if he has bent a bit more and caused himself pain and it appears that he is bending with all his might there is no need to be apprehensive.

"Prostration," how so? [27] After he raises himself and his head, [28] he sits down and falls on his face to the right and prays with all the supplication that he desires. It is prohibited to prostrate oneself on stones except in the Holy Temple, as it is explained in the tractate Abodah Zarah. [29] And a worthy man is not permitted to fall on his face except if he is convinced that he is as worthy as Joshua; [30] he rather lies down on his face but does not conceal his face in the soil. It is permissible for a person to pray in one place and fall on his face in another. One who prays with the congregation let him not extend his prayer more than necessary, but he may do so privately. And if he desires to recite after his prayers even the Order of the Confessional for the Day of Atonement, let him do so. Also if he has wished to add to each prayer of the "middle benedictions," supplications of similar content, let him add them. [31] If he has been ill or in need of sustenance, let him make additions according to his verbal ability, [32] but he should not supplicate in the first three benedictions or in the last three benedictions. One is prohibited to taste anything or do any work after dawn, until he prays. [33]

"Mutual greeting of scholars," how so? [34] The greeter says, "A good morning to you," and the one greeted replies, "A very good morning to you and may it last forever." The one who replies doubles the greeting.

The prayers were instituted in place of the "Daily Offerings" [35] as it is said, "Shall ye observe to offer unto Me in its due season" (Deut. 28:2). From this they instituted the "Stations," that they should stand watch over them. [36] Therefore a man should stand at the time that he recites the Eighteen Benedictions. One is obligated to answer "Amen" to each blessing, as it is written "Open ye the gates that the righteous nation that keepeth faithfulness may enter in" (Isa. 26:2), i.e., (the faithful) that say "Amen." [37]And greater is the merit of the one who answers "Amen" than he who blesses, because he affirms the blessings of the one who recites them. Also the one who blesses mentions only one Name, the one who answers "Amen" invokes two Names because "Amen" (91) totals the numerical value of *yod he vav he* (26) and *aleph daleth nun yod* (65).[38] And one must direct his heart towards heaven when answering "Amen," which is the abbreviation of *El Melekh Nehman*.[39] Talking and behaving light-headedly[40]is prohibited in the synagogue while standing before our King, Master of all the earth, blessed be His name. And woe unto the wicked who behave light-headedly, upon whom there is no fear of the Almighty; and there is neither fear nor reverence on their countenance and they will not discern or accept an example. "For pass over to the isles of the Kittites, and see, and consider diligently" that in all those lands the kings bend on their knees in their houses of prayer and they stand in awe, reverence and trembling and their hands spread out to their gods made by human hands which neither see nor hear. We who stand before the King of kings, the Holy One, blessed be He, eternal exalted and lifted up, blessed be His name and His fame be exalted, He to whom all praises are due, all the more must we stand before Him with awe and reverence, with fear and trembling. Concerning those who sit in the House of Prayer and appear to be exhausted and are unable to stand, concerning them the verse says, "Yet you did not call upon Me, O Jacob, but you have been weary of me, O Israel" (Isa. 43:22). All day he is not tired but during prayer he is tired.[41] The entire day he stands in the market before the officer, or before some scoffer and he is not weary, but during prayer he is unable to stand.

If one is praying and a prayer book has fallen before him to earth, if his mind is distracted from concentrating, and he is unable to pray with devotion, let him pick it up and pray with devotion. But before picking it up let him conclude the benediction which he has already begun. And if he is able to direct his mind let him not pick up the book which is on the ground, for he who prays with devotion shares in the world to come. Let a man always rise to attend the synagogue in order to merit being counted among the first ten, for even if a hundred come after him he is given reward equivalent to all of them.[42] A man who lives in a village and does not have ten people with whom to recite divine offices,[43] or lives in a place where there is a congregation and he has come late, after they have recited, "May His great name";[44] let him say, "Let the power of the Lord be great according as Thou hast spoken, saying" (Num. 14:17), "Thus will I magnify Myself, and sanctify Myself and I will make Myself known in the eyes of many nations, and they shall know that I am the Lord" (Ezek. 38:23), "Blessed be the name of the Lord from this time forth and forever" (Ps. 113:2).

Let a man not leave the synagogue until they complete the entire prayer service, except for the privy or to expectorate. In the evening close to prayer let a man not take a child to his bosom lest he soil his garments. Even if he wash them in water, they will not be as clean as before. Moreover, it is possible that while searching after the water the hour for *Minha* will have passed, or between and betwixt they will have recited the *Kaddish* with him being unable to respond with the "Amen." Moreover, perhaps the child will cry when he wishes to set him down and he will take pity on him and would not defer to the honor of his Owner and he will not go at all to the House of Assembly. "Create me a clean heart, O God," (Ps. 51:12) i.e., a man should not imagine an indecent or repulsive thought during prayer. Let him not touch these (indecent and repulsive) things during prayer. Let him not recite *Modim*[45] if there is saliva in his mouth. Let him not pray until the saliva is eliminated from his mouth. And if he has not recited the benedictions of *Ovos*[46] with devotion until *Mogen Abraham,* let him repeat it and pray again. And so with the recitation of *Shema* if he has not recited the first verse with devotion, let him repeat it in a whisper but let him not recite it in a loud voice, for it would appear as though two powers govern the universe.[47] A person who is unable to pray with devotion without a prayer book in which the prayer is written, or a person sated and unable to concentrate on the Blessings of Grace, let him read it from a book wherein the Blessings of Grace are inscribed. If he has not prayed with devotion, then when they pray quietly let him direct his heart with the reader and let him say each word with him. If you wonder about those who stammer in their speech and pronounce *het* as *heh* and *shin* as *samekh* and *kuf* as *teth* and *raish* as *daleth,* as to how they pray or how they read in the Torah and recite matters of holiness; when they reach the verse

24

(Ps. 33:20), *Nafshaynu Hikhtha,* are they not revilers and blasphemers?[48] Do not wonder about this matter, for our Creator, who searches hearts, does not seek anything but the heart of man that it be whole with Him, and although he cannot speak properly it is nevertheless as if he recites it properly. And so to those who read the "Verses of Praise"[49] in a loud voice and with melodious song and do not know the verses and recite them with error, their prayers and songs are accepted as savory odors. And also the Holy One, blessed be He, rejoices over him greatly and says, "How much he sings before Me according to his thinking." Concerning this it is said, "And His banner over me is love" (Cant. 2:4). His faithlessness to me is love. "His mouth trespasseth not in judgement" (Prov. 16:10); we translate, "He does not deceive with his mouth." It happened with a priest who with hands outstretched blessing the people said, *Yishmadkho* "let him destroy you." There was a scholar present who removed him from before the ark, because he did not know how to pronounce the letters in the Priestly Benediction. It was shown through heaven to this scholar that if he did not restore him he would be punished because of the matter. He who prays should focus his eyes downward and his heart upward[50] in order to fulfill those two passages, "And Mine eyes and Mine heart shall be there perpetually" (I Kings 9:3), "Let us lift our heart and our hands unto God in the heavens" (Lam. 3:41). And those who raise their heads and their eyes upward as one would look at the angels we deride and call heads of thorns.[51]

19. Twenty-four things interfere with repentance.[1] These are they: (1) gossiping evil, (2) slandering, (3) anger, (4) thinking evil, (5) fraternizing with the wicked, (6) eating at a table a meal that does not even suffice for the host, (7) staring at lewdness, (8) dividing spoils with a thief, (9) saying, "I will sin and the Day of Atonement will atone," (10) disregarding one's teachers, (11) cursing the community, (12) withholding the community from performing a meritorious deed is also included in this sin, (13) deflecting one's friend from a meritorious deed to an act of transgression, (14) making use of the poor man's pledge, (15) accepting bribes to pervert the law, (16) finding a lost object and not announcing it publicly so that it can be returned to its rightful owners, (17) seeing one's son going out to a

bad environment and not reprimanding him, (18) eating the plunder of the poor and widows, (19) separating oneself from the community, (20) transgressing the words of the sages, (21) honoring oneself at the expense of a friend's disgrace, (22) suspecting the innocent, (23) despising reproof, (24) scorning the commandments. All these twenty-four things withhold repentance. Repentance is not withheld if he has repented of them,[2] for he is then a penitent and has a share in the world to come.

And these things are differentiated in their various aspects. They are not all equal in punishment or with regard to repentance. There are aspects of them that close the path of repentance before their doers: "One who separates himself from the path of the community," that at the time that they do penance he will not be with them, and he will not share with them in the good deeds that they perform; "One who contests the words of the sages," because argument causes him to separate from them and he does not know repentance; "one who disregards his teachers," because this causes him to be banished from the world, and in the time that he is being driven from the world he will not find a teacher to show him the path of truth;[3] "One who mocks the commandments," since they are despised in his eyes he will never pursue them, will not love them and will not perform them; "One who abhors reproof," since he despises his reprover he will never find a reprover to lead him in the good path. Reproofs cause repentance, for at the time that they let the man know of his sin and shame him he then regrets his actions[4] and returns (to God) in repentance. And so we find with Moses when he would admonish Israel he would remind them of all their transgressions, "Ye have been rebellious" (Deut. 9:7), in order to cause them to repent, and (in this manner) all of the prophets reproved Israel. Therefore it is necessary to set up in each and all of Israel's communities a person, an elder, wise and God-fearing from his youth onward and beloved to the people of his city, to reprove them and return them (to God) in repentance. And this one despises reproof and does not listen to his words therefore he will remain in his sins, which in his eyes are good. There are things which are great transgressions and him who does one of them the Holy One, blessed be He, does not let repent because of the gravity of his sin. These are they: one who leads the community astray and included in this perversity is one who restrains the community from performing a meritorious act; one who leads his neighbor from a good to an evil path, such as an instigator and seducer. One who sees his son conducting an evil life and does not reprimand him and his son is still in his care. For if he were to reprimand him, he would mend his ways; this is therefore tantamount to causing him to sin. Included in this perversion is each one who has the power to rebuke others, both the community and individuals, and has not done so;[5] it is as though he placed the snare with his own hands; also he who says, "I will sin and repent," "I will sin and the Day of Atonement will atone." There are some things for which he who does them is unable to do complete penance, because they are between him and his fellow-man; for example, when he does not know the person against whom he has sinned in order to ask for his forgiveness or, if he has stolen, to whom to make restitution. These[6] are they: one who curses the community and has not cursed a specific individual, to be able to approach him, appease him and ask of him forgiveness; one who shares with a thief, because he does not know from whom the theft was taken because he[7] steals from all people and brings it to him and he accepts it therefore he doesn't know to whom to make restitution, moreover, he strengthens the hands of the thief and causes him to sin; one who finds a lost object and does not proclaim it in order to return it to the owners, after a while when he does make penance he does not know to whom to return it; one who eats the loot taken from poor people, orphans and widows, these unfortunate people are not known and wander from city to city and there is no one that knows them to know to whom to return it; he who accepts a bribe to pervert justice, he does not know the extent of the perversion and what loss is involved in order to make a proper restitution moreover, he strengthens the hand of the pervert and causes him to sin.

These are very bad things and he who does them in all probability will not return (to God) because they are simple in the eyes of most people and it appears to them that it is no perversion but it is a decisive sin and perversion. These are they: one who eats at the table a meal that does not even suffice for the host, which is a great sin but he who eats thinks in his heart, "What is my sin, I ate only with his permission"; he who uses the pledge of the poor man, for instance he loans to the poor man on his ax and the creditor chops wood without the poor man's permission and says, "What is my sin if I have chopped with it, he loses nothing thereby."[8] One who stares at lewdness, thinks in his heart, "What is my transgression, wherein is my sin, if I did look at my kinsman have I then fornicated with her?" He does not know or understand that he causes sin to the person involved, as it is written, "That ye go not about after your own heart and your own eyes after which ye used to go astray" (Num. 15:39). And in the book of Ben Sira he says, "Avert your eyes from a beautiful woman."[9]

The rabbis commented on the verse, "He shutteth his eyes from looking on evil" (Isa. 33:15), that he closes his eyes from looking at women.[10] A woman's leg is a sexual incitement.[11] The voice of a woman is indecency.[12] As our sages have said, "He who stares at the small finger of a woman is as if staring at the pudenda."[13] They also have said, "Even at the colored clothing of a woman stretched out on the wall, if he recognizes the owner he is prohibited from looking."[14]

He who honors himself through the shame of his neighbor says in his heart he is not sinning in that he does not embarrass him and did not bring him to his shame. In what manner does he do this? He compares his deeds with his neighbor's wisdom, and his wisdom with the deeds of his friend, in order that it may appear therefrom that he is honored and his friend disgraced.

To him "who suspects the innocent," it appears that he is not sinning, but he needs to learn from Moses, our teacher, who spoke evil and suspected the innocent in that he said, "But behold they will not believe me" (Exod. 4:1), (and) immediately he was stricken with leprosy.[15] There are five things to which he who does them will remain addicted and from which he will find it difficult to separate himself. Therefore a man must beware of them and remove himself in order not to cleave to them, for they are extremely bad. And these are they: talking evil, going about tale-bearing, anger, thinking evil and associating with a wicked person because he learns from his ways, and they are marked in his heart, "But the companion of fools shall smart for it" (Prov. 13:20).[16]

20. Every commandment of the Law, both positive and negative, if a man transgresses one of them through error or deliberately, if he repents and returns from his sins he is enjoined to confess before God, may His name be exalted, as it is written, "When a man or woman shall commit any sin that men commit, to commit a trespass . . . then they shall confess their sin" (Num. 5:6). This is a verbal confession and it involves a positive commandment. In what manner does one confess? He says, "I pray, O Lord, I have sinned, I have done perversely, I have transgressed before Thee, such and such have I done, and behold I am sorry, I am ashamed of my actions and I will never return to this thing."[1] This is the essence of the confession. And he who adds to his confession and elaborates in the matter is all the more praiseworthy.[2] And so sinners and the guilty at the time that they bring sacrifices for their sins and for their errors are not forgiven until they do penance and make a verbal confession, as it is written, "And he shall confess that wherein he hath sinned" (Lev. 5:5). And so all those under sentence of death by the court and those subject to lashes, their death and flagellation does not obtain forgiveness for them unless they do penance and confess.[3] And so he who wounds his neighbor or does damage to his neighbor even though he has paid him that which was due him is not atoned for until he confesses and returns from ever doing this again, as it is written, "Any sin that men commit" (Num. 5:6).[4] The goat that is to be sent away[5] atones for all transgressions in the Torah, light ones and more serious ones, both if the person transgressed in error and if he transgressed deliberately, both if it was made known to him or not made known to him, all is expiated for by the goat that is sent away and this all applies only when he does penance. But if he has not done penance the goat does not atone except for the light ones.[6] And which are the light ones and which are the more serious ones? The more serious ones are those for which one is guilty of the death penalty or of excision (from Israel). A needless oath and a false oath, even though excision is not applicable, are considered among the more serious ones. And all other positive commandments and negative commandments which do not involve excision are regarded as light ones. And in our day when the Holy

29

Temple no longer exists and we have no atonement through the altar there is nothing left but penance. Penance atones for all transgressions. Even if a man has been wicked all his days and has done penance at the end, his wickedness is not counted, as it is written, "And as for the wickedness of the wicked he shall not stumble thereby in the day thereby he turneth from his wickedness" (Ezek. 33:12).[7] And the gravity of the Day of Atonement atones for penitents, as it is written, "For on this day shall atonement be made for you" (Lev. 16:30).[8] Even though repentance atones and the gravity of the Day of Atonement atones, there are transgressions which obtain forgiveness only after a time.[9] How so? A man has transgressed a positive commandment not involving excision and has done penance he does not go away from there until he is forgiven. Concerning these (such transgressors) it is said, "Return, ye backsliding children, I will heal your backslidings" (Jer. 3:22). If a man has transgressed a negative commandment which does not involve excision and capital punishment and has repented, the repentance suspends judgement and the Day of Atonement atones. Concerning this it is said, "For on this day shall atonement be made" (Lev. 16:30). If he has transgressed in a matter involving excision and capital punishment and has done penance, penance and the Day of Atonement suspend judgement and the tribulations that visit him conclude the expiation, and he never does obtain full forgiveness until tribulation comes upon him. Concerning them (such transgressors) Scripture says, "Then will I visit their transgression with the rod and their iniquity with strokes" (Ps. 89:33). When does this apply? Only when he did not profane the Name when he transgressed, for example, he committed the transgression in secret (is expiation possible), but profaning the Name publicly, even though he has done penance and the Day of Atonement has arrived and he stands yet within his penance and tribulation has visited him, not even all of these are able to cleanse his wrong so as to obtain (for him) full forgiveness, except that he die. Repentance, the Day of Atonement and tribulations, these three only suspend judgement but death cleanses and atones, as it is said, "And the Lord of hosts revealed Himself in mine ears" (Isa. 22:14).

What is complete penance? (It is illustrated by) one to whom a transgression has presented itself which he has already transgressed and he has the opportunity to do it again but has withdrawn and has not done it because of the penance and not because of fear or weakness. How so? Behold one who has cohabited illicitly with a woman and later has been left alone again with her and has had the opportunity to do it again, and he has been still steadfast in his love for her and has been able to do it, but has subdued his passion and has not transgressed, he is a complete penitent. Concerning this one Solomon said, "Remember then thy Creator in the days of thy youth" (Eccl. 12:1).[10] And if he has not returned except in his old age and at the time when it is no longer possible because of his failing strength, to do that which he was able to do in his youth, even though this is not the best penance it avails, and he is regarded as a penitent. And even though he has transgressed all his life and at the end, at the time of his death, he has repented and he has died penitent, all of his transgressions are forgiven him,[11] as it is said, "Before the sun and the light . . . are darkened" (Eccl. 12:2), which is the day of death, from which we can deduce that if he remembers his Creator before death he is forgiven. And what is this repentance? That the sinner forsake his sin and remove evil thoughts from his heart, and resolve in his heart to do it (the evil) no more, as it is said, "Let the wicked forsake his way" (Isa. 55:7). Let him repent and regret his previous sins, as it is written, "Surely after that I was turned I repented" (Jer. 31:18); and let him say, "I give testimony concerning myself before Him Who knows all hidden things, that I will not return to this sin ever; as it is written, "Neither will we call anymore the work of our hands our gods" (Hos. 14:4).[12] And in keeping with the paths of repentance it would have been proper for him to cry continuously before God with weeping and supplications, do charity according to his ability, further himself greatly from the things wherein he sinned, change his name, that is to imply, that "I am another and not that man who did those evil things," and he changes his actions for the good to rear himself in the upright path. He imposes exile upon himself because exile atones for transgression, it subdues him and causes him to become humble and meek. And it is most praiseworthy for the penitent to confess publicly and let his sin be known and reveal his sin that is between him and his neighbor to others, saying to them, "I have sinned against so and so and such and such have I done to him and this day I return and do penance." And the proud who do not make known but conceal their sins, their repentance is not complete, as it is written, "He that covereth his transgression shall not prosper; but who so confesseth and forsaketh shall obtain mercy" (Prov. 28:13). In what case (who so confesseth . . . shall obtain mercy)? Only (in cases) concerning transgressions between man and man, but involving those between man and his Master, he does not need to publicize them. It is insolence on his part if he has revealed it to another; instead he returns to his Creator, blessed be He, and enumerates his sins before Him but confesses them before the congregation inexplicitly, (saying) "I have sinned." It is best that he not reveal his transgressions, "Happy is he whose transgression is forgiven, whose sin is pardoned" (Ps. 32:1).[13]

21. The pious men of olden days were wont to write their transgressions on a tablet when they sinned in order to confess their sins,[1] also in order to remember, regret and do penance. Because if he remembers his transgressions and that in the future he must give an accounting of them,[2] he will do penance, therefore it is good to record them, to fulfill that which is written, "And my sin is ever before me" (Ps. 51:5). And he remembers the day of death, Gehenna, and the day of judgement and lastly the love of heaven which is the best.[3] Let him write them cryptically in order that nobody sees them. The statement of the rabbis that one who declares his sins is called "impudent," refers to one who enumerates his sins, who tells everyone wherein he sinned. But one is permitted to tell a humble and righteous individual one of his transgressions, that he may be able to teach him how to do penance. Or he should inquire of him inexplicitly, "If a person has committed such a transgression and comes to repent, how does he do penance?" Even though penance and weeping are good for the person at all times, the days between the New Year and the Day of Atonement are better,[4] and they (penance and weeping) are immediately accepted, as it is written, "Seek ye the Lord while He may be found" (Isa. 55:6). This is said only concerning the individual, but with the community, as long as they are doing penance and crying with whole hearts, they are answered, as in a similar matter where it is written, "For what great nation is there, that hath God so nigh unto them, as the Lord our God is whensoever we call upon

Him?" (Deut. 4:7) The Day of Atonement is the day of penance for each individual and the community, it is the time of remission and pardon for all Israel. Therefore, all are enjoined to do penance and to confess on the Day of Atonement. And the commandment concerning confession on the Day of Atonement is that it start while yet day before the individual eats or drinks lest he choke. Let him recite the confessional that is customary "But we have sinned," and this is the quintessence of the Confessional. Transgressions, even though he has confessed them on the Day of Atonement and he is yet within a state of penance, them he confesses on another Day of Atonement, as it is written, "For I know my transgression: and my sin is ever before me" (Ps. 51:5). [5]

22. He who has sinned in a matter and others are suspected (of it), must say, "I am the one that has sinned," in order that the world not sin because of him in suspecting the innocent. [1] And if he be in the company of people and something improper is done and it is not known who is the sinner, he must say, "I am the one that has sinned," even though he did not sin. For through his confession the sinner will not be shamed, as it happened with Rabbi Meir, "It happened with a certain woman who came to the academy of Rabbi Meir that she said to them, "One of you betrothed me with intercourse." Rabbi Meir stood up and wrote a divorce document and gave it to her and so did all. [2] And he who confesses for others is able to say, "We have sinned," and to include himself with them because all Israelites are guarantors for each other. [3] And if he saw people sinning and did not reprove them he should confess even though he did not sin. [4] And when he confesses let him recall all of his sins as they are. If he does not repent of a part of his transgressions let him say, "You are our Creator and You know our inclinations and You will humble the passions of our heart and circumcize our uncircumcision that our neck be not stiffened any more."

23. Repentance and the Day of Atonement atone only for transgressions between man and his Master, [1] for example, one who has eaten something prohibited or has indulged in prohibited cohabitation or the like. But for transgressions between man and his fellow-man such as bruising or cursing or robbing and the like, one is never forgiven until he returns the thing that he owes, and appeases

33

the other.[2] Even though he has returned the money that he owes him, he must appease him and seek his forgiveness,[3] and even if he has enraged his friend only with words,[4] he must pacify him and entreat him until he is forgiven. If his friend refuses and is unwilling to forgive him, he shall bring a group of people who will appeal fervently in his behalf and ask that he be forgiven. If the aggrieved is unwilling to acquiesce to them, he then shall bring a second and third group each consisting of three persons. If he is reconciled fine, if not he takes leave of him[5] (the aggrieved). And he who refuses to forgive is a sinner, for a man is prohibited from being so merciless as to be beyond pacification.[6] One must rather be difficult to anger and easy to pacify. And in the hour that the sinner seeks forgiveness from him he should forgive with a whole heart and eager spirit. Even if he has tormented him greatly and has sinned grievously, he shall not take vengeance nor bear any grudge.[7]

24. This is the path of the upright with their steadfast hearts, but the gentiles with their uncircumcised hearts are not so,[1] and their wrath is kept forever. Concerning the Gibeonites, because they have not forgiven and have remained unpacified, Scripture says, they "Were not of the children of Israel" (II Sam. 21:2).[2] He who has sinned against his teacher and seeks his pardon but is not pardoned, returns even a hundred times until he is pardoned.[3]

25. If someone has sinned against his neighbor and the neighbor dies before extending forgiveness, he (then) brings ten people, places them on his grave and says before them, "I have sinned before God, the God of Israel and against this individual to whom I have done such and such," and if he owes him money he returns it to his heirs, if he does not know who the heirs are, let him leave it with the court and confess.[1]

26. "Let your garments be always white" (Eccl. 9:8). He should always regard himself as if about to die, and perhaps he will die soon thus dying in sin,[1] therefore let him repent immediately of his sin, as it is written "Repent one day before thy death, etc." Therefore let him repent one day before his death, for one hour in repentance is good.[2]

27. Do not say that one need not search his ways and repent but from transgressions which entail action, such as robbing, un-

chastity, stealing and the like. But as the individual must withdraw and repent of these, so must he search out evil thoughts and repent of them, such as anger, enmity, jealousy, mockery and pursuing gluttony and the like. Of all these he must repent. And these are more difficult than transgressions which possess action. For when a man is habituated in these, it is difficult to withdraw from them after he has become sunken and accustomed to acting. Concerning this it is said "Let the wicked forsake his ways" (Isa. 55:7).

28. This is the instruction to one who repents with all his heart with all his soul and with all his might in order to cleave to his Creator.[1] For each and every transgression which presents itself, he should consider, what if, God forbid, they were to force baptism upon him, he would rather let himself be killed for the Unity of the Name. If this (baptism), which is so difficult (to) withstand he does withstand in His Name, then all other transgressions would be easily put aside. And as soon as one comes to purify himself he is helped from Heaven.[2] If a man experiences unchaste thoughts about a certain woman during his prayer or other impure fancies, let him dig his thumbs into the earth and let him "hang his body upon them"[3] and not lean against a wall and this will dispel the impure fancies. If he is sitting and is unable to rise because of people let him dig his thumbs vigorously into the earth. If a man is in the bathhouse or in a polluted place and thoughts of love possess his heart, or a woman passes before him, let him meditate on matters of Torah[4] because Torah is good to purify the heart of its evil inclination.[5] Even though it is permissible to meditate on Torah everywhere except in the bathhouse and privy, nevertheless to withdraw a man from transgression it is permitted.[6] And let a man avoid coming to nocturnal pollution by not drinking more wine then is suited, because it afflicts his heart and turns him aside from God, as it is written, "Harlotry, wine and new wine take away the heart" (Hos. 4:11). And if a transgression presents itself to him, let him pray with all his heart to his Creator that He rescue him. And if the individual were to be visited with tribulations he would presently fast, cry and pray to his Creator, all the more so should a man pray to his Creator that He rescue him from transgression.[7] And let a man not acquire for himself

35

a prosecutor on the Day of Judgement. All transgressions committed in this world, each and everyone, envelop him and lead him to Judgement Day, as it is written, "The paths of their way do wind" (Job 6:18).

29. If an individual stood steadfast in a meritorious deed let him not boast of it saying, "How pious I am." But rather let him offer praise and thanks to the Lord, praised and exalted be His fame, Who has rescued him from sinning before Him, who has it in His power to incline the heart to all that He desires, as it is written, "The king's heart is in the hand of the Lord as the watercourses" (Prov. 21:1). And he says, "and I also withheld thee from sinning against Me" (Gen. 20:6). Each one who wishes to return in repentance and achieve a status of piety and fathom the depths of God's law, the depths of His glory, let him not enter (attempt to do so) except if he be discerning and a soul of goodwill without anger. Let him forsake converse with people and playing with children, [1] also converse with his wife except during coitus. [2] And let him be as careful in the observance of a light command as a more serious command, [3] and on guard to rise before an elder even a hundred times. And let this not be as a burden upon him because of his love for the Creator.

30. Beware, watch your soul lest you be captured in the domain of the evil inclination, lest it thrust you aside from the land of the living. He who seduces you to commit a lesser evil and one who draws your heart to a graver one, [1] humble him and suppress him that he be given over into your hand and not that you be given over into his hand, lest he bring you to the lowest pit with fire unblown. And thine evil inclination will not be given over into your hand, but through repentance to your Creator. And to further yourself from the flesh of lust, remember the days which are to come and the great good stored up, "And if thou doest well shall it not be lifted up? And if thou doest not well sin coucheth at the door." [2] And you, son of man, return to your Maker with all your heart, and set your heart aright with Him who tries your mind. Raise up your eyes to the heavens and let it shine upon you with joy. Let not your evil inclination trip you during your life. Each day and night return to your heart. For after death there are the afflictions of the grave and after that the bitter judgement of Gehenna. For bitterly do they weep, that

they (in Gehenna) be given strength to endure the intensity of the afflictions.[3] And even after he has been rescued from the judgement of Gehenna there are still other judgements difficult and bitter.[4] Also the worms that come out of your flesh will eat your carcass and our sages said the worms are as painful for the dead as a needle in the flesh of the living.[5]

31. At all times you should love your Creator with all your heart and all your soul and take counsel with your heart and a lesson from man who is but worms; if a person gives you ten gold pieces or more, how deeply engraved would his love be in your heart. And if he provides your support and the support of your children and of your household you would certainly think, "This man which I have never seen and who has extended to me such kindness I would not be able to repay for all the goodness he has shown me should I live a thousand years. I would love him with all my heart and with all my soul; he could not command me to do anything that I would not do for him, because both my wealth and my being are his." As with the love of man so with the love of the Holy One, blessed be He, raised and exalted be His fame. It is He who gives sustenance to all, how much better that we should cleave to the love of the Creator, fear Him, nor transgress His commands whether great or small. For we do not know the reward of each commandment,[1] and the punishment for transgressions though they appear light in our eyes, as it is written, "When the iniquity of my supplanters compasseth me about" (Ps. 49:6). The transgressions to which a man becomes habituated in this world will encompass him on the Day of Judgement.[2] If he is deserving his good deeds will bear witness for him.[3] True and firm it is that we are not to transgress the commandments of our Creator even one of the small ones for a house full of gold and silver. If an individual says, "I will transgress a commandment and with the gold and silver they give me I will fulfill the difficult commandments. With this I will support the poor, invite wayfarers, I will do very many favors." These are all futile thoughts, for perhaps soon after the transgression he will die and not succeed to the gift. Moreover, if he should not die the money would soon be dissipated so that he dies

in his sin. Come and see how much you should love your Creator who does wonderful kindnesses with you, He creates you from a decayed drop, He gives you a soul, draws you forth from the belly, then gives you a mouth with which to speak, a heart to understand, ears to hear the pure words of His mouth, which are refined as silver and pure gold. It is He who leads you on the face of earth, who gives sustenance to all, who causes death and gives life to all. In His hand are the souls of all the living. It is He who distributes your share of bread. What is there to say? for the mouth is unable to speak, the ear unable to hear, for to Him all praise is as silence, there is no end to the length of His days, His years will have no end, He is the King of kings, the Holy One, blessed be His name and His fame. It is He who has created the heavens and earth, sea, and all that is therein. He is the provider of all, for His eyes are open upon all men's paths recompensing each according to his ways and the fruit of his deeds, whether good or bad. Behold it is He who sets forth before men two paths, the path of life and the path of death and says to you, "Choose life" (Deut. 30:19). In spite of all this, we who are filled with worms do not think and do not set our hearts but to fill our appetites freely. We do not think that man's days are numbered,[4] today he is here, tomorrow in the grave,[5] that suddenly he dies. For no man rules over his spirit [6] retaining it (forever). Therefore it is good for man to remove himself from all appetites and direct his heart to love and fear the Lord with all his heart at all times and to revile the life of vanity. For we will not be able to humble ourselves and subdue our passion which thrusts us from the land of the living, except through subduing our heart and returning to our Maker in complete repentance, to serve Him and to do His will with a whole heart. Our sages have said, "Bread and salt shalt thou eat and water in measurement shall you drink [7] and beware of gazing at women which drives a person from the world.[8] Love humans[9] and judge all people in the scale of merit."[10] And this is what the Torah has said, "But in righteousness shalt thou judge thy neighbor" (Lev. 19:15). Be humble before all, busy yourself with Torah, which is whole, pure and upright and do not praise yourself for it, because for this were you created.[11]

32. Each man who loves virtue, loves reproofs, loves reprimands, loves acts of charity, invites the wayfarer and recites his prayers with

devotion, such a man, even if his dwelling be outside the Holy Land, will not be visited with the afflictions of the grave.[1] And even the judgement of Gehenna he does not see. Come and see how your heart would rejoice if a king of flesh and blood were to say to you, "Serve before me," even though he is a worm like yourself. And we who serve the King of kings, the Holy One, blessed be He, how much more should we rejoice and be zealous in the service of the Holy One, blessed be He. And so they have said, "Be strong as a tiger, light as an eagle, swift as a deer and as mighty as a lion to do the will of your Father in heaven."[2] "The end of the matter, all having been heard: fear God for this is the whole man" (Eccl. 12:13).

33. "Out of the mouth of the Most High proceedeth not evil and good?" (Lam. 3:38). The Holy One, blessed be He, does not decree that a man be either good or bad.[1] And so the scholars have said, "All is in the hands of Heaven except the fear of Heaven"[2] as it is has been said, "And now, Israel, what doth the Lord thy God, require of thee but to fear..."(Deut. 10:12). In the hour that a person is born, it is decreed whether he will be strong or weak, rich or poor, handsome or ugly, tall or short, but not whether he will be righteous or wicked,[3] they merely place before him two paths and he chooses one. And since this sinner injures himself when he turns from the good path, eschewing the good and choosing evil, he therefore needs to cry and wail for that which he has done to his soul. His reward is evil, and this is as it has been written after it, "Wherefore doth living man complain, a strong man because of his sins" (Lam. 3:39). Come and see how numerous are the afflictions, the fasts and the supplications entreated when his son or one of his loved ones is sick, for then his heart is bitter. So much the more must he afflict himself and mourn when he commits a transgression. Repentance returns his soul to two worlds.[4]

34. "May the Lord cut off all flattering lips, The tongue that speaketh proud things!" (Ps. 12:4). He who relates evil gossip is regarded as if he had denied God,[1] for it is written after that, they "who have said: 'Our tongue will we make mighty: Our lips are with us: who is our lord over us?'" (Ps. 12:5). Gossip, which knows no limit, see how powerful it is, and let us take a lesson from the "spies."[2] Even when one slanders wood and stones, which do not hear and see,

there is concern for their shame, so much more when one slanders his neighbor who is created in the (divine) image and likeness, "What shall be given thee, and what shall be done more unto thee, Thou deceitful tongue" (Ps. 1:23). The Holy One, blessed be He has said to the tongue, "What shall I do to you? All of man's limbs are from without, you are within. Moreover, I have made for you two walls, one of bone and one of flesh; of bone, the teeth; and of flesh, the lips." "In the multitude of words there wanteth not transgression" (Prov. 10:19). A man should always increase (his) silence [3] and not speak at all, except (to indulge) in the words of the wise or in matters necessary for the needs of his body. It has been said of Rav, the student of Rabenu (Judah) the Pious, that in all his days he never indulged in idle talk.[4] All who indulge in ordinary talk transgress a positive commandment as it has been said, "And shalt talk of them (Deut. 6:7) and not in other matters."[5] And (we know) that a prohibition which has been derived by implication from a positive command is a positive command.[6] Others say, he violates both a prohibition and a positive command, as it is said, "all things toil to weariness; man cannot utter it . . . " (Eccl. 1:8). And even involving bodily needs, let his words not be excessive, but sparing, and concern only those matters which are deemed necessities.[7] And so with words of Torah let a man's talk be brief and the content great. For so have the scholars said, "let a man always teach his students by way of the short method."[8] But if his words are many and the content meagre, it is then foolishness, as it is written, "And a fool's voice through a multitude of words" (Eccl. 5:2). A safeguard to wisdom is silence.[9] Therefore let a man not be hasty in answering[10] nor speak excessively. Also let him teach his student with composure and quietness, without shouting or lengthiness, for "the words of the wise (are) spoken in quiet" (Eccl. 9:17).

35. He who speaks and is concerned only with his own words and does not consider God[1] Who knows his thoughts, his very coming and going Who counts his steps and before Whose glory and power his words are laid, as it is written, "Can any hide himself in secret places that I shall not see him? Saith the Lord. Do not I fill heaven and earth? Saith the Lord" (Jer. 23:23); this man is not on a good path. For the nature of man should be to think of his Creator con-

tinually and to place Him before himself, as it is written, "I have set the Lord always before me" (Ps. 16:8). When a man sits in solitude, wherever he may be, let him empty his mind of all vain matters and think only of his Creator, of His holiness and wonders and of His favors which He does for us each day. But when a despised man concentrates on idle things or hears vain matters, even though he does not intend to speak, immediately he turns his thoughts to idleness[2] with loss to himself for each and every good thought which (rightfully) should be thought of his Creator's holiness and of His fear so pure. He should be in that good, pure and exalted station to **worship God for love and desire of His commands.** And this is the grand worship that the ministering angels and the hosts of heaven, who declaim His holiness, employ as it is said, "Holy, holy, holy" (Isa. 6:3). Therefore one needs to be careful and not multiply idle talk lest he forget the Lord who is always before him, as the seeing before the blind (so is He) with His presence and strength in all places. And this blind man is one who does not see except through his vain thoughts and does not remember the Lord and removes himself from the standard of truth and fear of Him. For it (fear of God) is not found in his heart because of the hardness of his heart, which is calloused and distant from God, in his mind are found only vain thoughts. Therefore he is not present in the Divine Mind, only through difficulty and force. As the blind person cannot perceive or apprehend the person who is before him if he does not touch him or hear his voice, so too an individual cannot learn and bind God in his heart permanently unless he forsake transgression. For transgressions divide and darken fear of the Lord and change one's countenance[3] and so he says, "But your iniquities have separated between you and your God" (Isa. 59:2).

36. In the fullness of silence there is reverence.[1] He who fears God, obeys Him, sees Him, knows Him and searches for Him and is silent because of his fear, is the one who adds to (His) reverence. But if he heightens and raises his voice he diminishes reverence, for he forgets that he stands before God as a blind man who stands before a king. He multiplies words without fearing him, because he does not see whom to fear. He who increases silence because of reverence will not soon come to sin.

41

37. "The fear of the Lord is clean" (Ps. 19:10). There is no equivocation. A person who finds an occasion to sin (in a situation) where there is no cause to fear others or risk of being shamed and does not permit himself to sin because of fear of God, reflects the essence of reverence. And if he has done so many times, but once succumbed to his evil inclination and did sin, he does not forfeit his other merits. Let neither his hands nor heart weaken from continuing to do good.[1] But if he regrets and is sorry for his previous deeds he receives no reward for his troubles in subduing his evil inclination initially. Concerning this it is said, "But when the righteous turneth away from his righteousness, and committeth iniquity" (Ezek. 18:24) none of his righteous deeds shall be remembered.

38. "Keep thy tongue from evil" (Ps. 34:14) when you reprove your neighbor guard your money.[1] He whose words exceed his wisdom, his words will be upon him. He whose wisdom exceeds his words, let his words be with him.[2] This means, he whose words and reproofs of others exceed his understanding, that is to say, he is neither wise nor understanding enough to do as he says and his understanding does not prevail upon him to act in accord with his good words, his words will disgrace him. For listeners will say to everyone, "These virtues for which he reproves us, he himself lacks; he preaches well but does not act as well."[3] But one whose wisdom exceeds his words, who does not reprove excessively, but only according to the dictates of reason, wisdom, conduct and the loftiest virtues which are within him, his words will be with him, that is to say, the virtues for which he reproves others will be for him an honor and adornment. Listeners will say, "All this wisdom and discipline of which he speaks can all be found in him." This is to teach you that silence is better than excessive talk. For the increase of silence redowns to one's honor and grace, but excessive talk is a disgrace and shame. Of necessity, he who studies the book of Hasiduth and wisdom will try to act to the extent that he is able to understand, and will not aspire to understand merely to know a book. Merely to relate wisdom serves no purpose for the one who does so, it does not endure except with the one who absorbs it and only then is it of use to the one who relates it. Another explanation of "his words exceed his understanding,"

is that he says more than is appropriate for him in light of his (own limited) wisdom and understanding. Solomon has said, "Overbearing speech becometh not a churl" (Prov. 17:7), then his words will rule over him and he will be caught in their hands. "He whose understanding exceeds his words," i.e., that his wisdom is greater and in excess of his words, is virtuous. From his abundant wisdom he governs his spirit and does not bring words forth except in keeping with his judgement and understanding. His words will be heard, that is to say, they are his and in his possesssion, as "My beloved is mine and I am his" (Cant. 2:16).

39. "A time to keep silence and a time to speak" (Eccl. 3:7) (refers to) when they revile, curse him and say ignoble things (about him), there is (then) to be no reply. "And a time to speak," also refers to when they speak in matters of Law, then is not a time to keep silent.[1] (Another interpretation) also "A time to keep silence," is not to reprimand those whom you know will not accept reproof in the slightest matter.[2] For it is better that they act inadvertently rather than transgress willfully. "And a time to speak," (refers to) when you are able to protest and your words are heard.

40. "May, but for Thy sake are we killed all the day" (Ps. 44:23). These are people who suffer insult and shame because of the commandments. For when one tells a person it is foolish to fulfill the commandments of fringes and phylacteries and the like, his blood spills as water because of the shame. Scripture regards this as if he had been murdered because of it. One who shames another is regarded as a murderer[1] and it (sin) withholds him from performing a meritorious deed. This is what Scripture has said, "That make a man an offender by words" (Isa. 29:21) and it has been said, "Because for Thy sake I have borne reproach" (Ps. 69:8). "Still greater is the effect of shame," our sages have said, "in the case of one who commits a sin and is put to shame by it, he is pardoned for all his transgressions."[2] For it is said, "That thou mayest remember and be confounded and never open thy mouth anymore because of thy shame when I have forgiven thee all that thou hast done, saith the Lord, God" (Ezek. 16:63).

41. If not for "shame," which God created, no one would be free of transgression. Proof of this is that it is more common to murder

a person openly than to sleep openly with a woman, even (one's) own wife. For anger is found in each person, the great, small and elderly alike; but the evil inclination is found only in youths, but not in the small, elderly or the weak. And those youths whose evil inclination overwhelms them are not let off therefrom except because of shame.[1] Therefore an individual cannot boast if he has done good and has not sinned since in his youth he was restrained by his parents or by his shame; therefore even if in later life he avoids sin, let him not boast, since he had initially recoiled from sin because of shame.

42. Repentance needs four things;[1] first that he repent for each and every sin, transgression and offense. Secondly, that he forsake them. Thirdly, that he confess them in his heart. Fourthly, that he take upon himself with a whole heart, and resolve in his heart that he will not return to do them (sins) again, lest he appear as one undergoing purification with an unclean creature in his hand.[2] For repentance is of no avail to him until he casts the creature from his hand. Also he needs to single out the sin, as it is written, "O, this people have sinned a great sin and have made them a god of gold" (Exod. 32:31). And so should he confess, "I pray Thee, O God, I have sinned, I have done perversely, I have transgressed before Thee, I have done such and such, I am sorry I am ashamed of my deeds. And I give witness concerning myself, He who knows all hidden secrets, that I am resolved in my heart not to return to do this again."[3] And so it is written, "Turn Thou me God unto Thee and we will return for Thou are the Lord my God. Surely after that I was turned, I repented, and after that I was instructed, I smote upon my thigh; I was ashamed, yea, even confounded because I did bear the reproach of my youth" (Jer. 31:17).

43. For twenty-four offenses an individual is excommunicated, be it man or woman.[1] They are as follows: (1) one who spurns a messenger of the court;[2] (2) one who degrades a wise man even after his death;[3] (3) one who calls his neighbor "slave";[4] (4) one who treats lightly even one word of rabbinical law, let alone, biblical law;[5] (5) one who was summoned by the messenger of the court to appear in court at a given date, and did not come;[6] (6) one who does not accept the court's decision is excommunicated until he responds;[7] (7) one who harbors something that can do harm, such as

44

a dangerous dog, a defective ladder, is excommunicated until the menace is removed;[8] (8) one who sells land to a gentile (adjacent to that of an Israelite's) is excommunicated until he accepts liability for all accidents (damages) caused by the gentile to the Israelite residing next door;[9] (9) one who testifies against a Jew in gentile courts and is awarded money not in accord with Jewish law, is placed under the ban until he repays;[10] (10) a butcher who is a priest and does not set aside the prescribed gifts[11] and give them to another priest, is excommunicated until he does so;[12] (11) one who desecrates the second day of the holy days[13] observed by those living abroad, even though it be a custom;[14] (12) one who performs work on the eve of Passover after midday;[15] (13) one who invokes God's name in vain, or for an oath in inane matters;[16] (14) one who causes the community to profane God's name;[17] (15) one who causes the community to eat consecrated offerings outside its authorized place;[18] (16) one who calculates the years and institutes the new months outside the Holy Land;[19] (17) one who causes the blind to stumble;[20] (18) one who withholds the community from performing a meritorious deed;[21] (19) a butcher who is found with "Trefah";[22] (20) a butcher who does not examine his knife before a scholar;[23] (21) one who induces an erection;[24] (22) one who divorces his wife and then enters into a partnership or business with her which brings them together, when they come to the court they are put under ban;[25] (23) a scholar with a bad reputation;[26] (24) one who excommunicates another needlessly is himself deserving of excommunication.[27]

44. Four groups do not receive the Divine Presence:[1] a group of liars; a group of hypocrites; a group of gossipers; a group of scoffers; and all are referred to in Scripture. "A group of liars" (is denied the Divine Presence because it is stated) "He that speaketh falsehood shall not be established before Mine eyes" (Ps. 101:7). And also in the wars of Ahab, when he came and asked the prophets if he should go out and do battle, the spirit of Naboth came before God, and he said: "I will go forth and be a lying spirit in the mouth of all his prophets. And He said: etc. . . . 'Go forth'" (I Kings 22:22). And our scholars explain this to mean, "Go forth from my precincts."[2] "Hypocrites" (are denied His presence as it is written), "A hypocrite cannot come before Him" (Job 13:16). "Those who relate evil gossip" (are denied His

presence), for it is said, "For Thou art not a God that hath pleasure in wickedness; Evil shall not sojourn with Thee" (Ps. 5:5). Evil (doers) shall not sojourn with you nor enter your precincts. "Scoffers" (are denied His presence) "The boasters shall not stand in Thy sight" (Ps. 5:6). People who are scoffers confound the world. "Evil gossip," (includes also that which is) intended to dishonor his neighbor, even though it be true. [3] Even if it becomes a (popular) by-word, it is ignoble to indulge in its use. If one has spread an evil report about his neighbor or has disgraced him with reviling matters of which he had never been suspected and which no one had anticipated (but which were apparently true), the sin of the person who has revealed it is not atoned for, because he cannot set aright that which he has perverted, nor undo the disgrace caused his neighbor, and this is what Solomon said in his wisdom, "Lest he that heareth it revile thee" (Prov. 25:10). And so is it taught in the Jerusalem Talmud, [4] "He who sins against his neighbor, and then repeatedly goes and asks for his pardon, but his neighbor does not respond, let him form lines of people and pacify him before them. This is what is said, "He cometh before men and saith, 'I have sinned' against so and so and behold I repent." And if he does so, he redeems his soul from death, for it is written after that, "So He redeemeth his soul from going into the pit" (Job 33:28). Rabbi Jose said, "This is said concerning one who does not spread evil reports about his neighbor, but if he does there is absolutely no forgiveness." If he inflicts pain on an individual it is as though he inflicts pain on the entire world, for everything that is in the world is in man. [5] If he spits before him but the spittle does not reach him, he is free from judgement in human law, but guilty under divine law. [6] Even if he inflicts a small measure of pain he will be punished at the hands of the Lord for each and every hurt which he inflicts upon his neighbor, for it is said, "That for all these things God will bring thee into judgement (Eccl. 11:9) concerning every hidden thing" (Eccl. 12:14). And our rabbis elucidate, [7] "What is meant with 'concerning every hidden thing'?" This refers to one who kills vermin before his neighbor and disgusts him thereby, others say it refers to one who spits. Therefore all the God-fearing and righteous through whom the Holy One, blessed be He, does not cause any stumbling, let them be cautious to forgive immediately those who kill vermin or spit or do anything repulsive so that there be no stumbling through them (the righteous).[8] It is reported of a certain pious man that he covered all the spittle that he found in a place where he knew the offender to be a Jew and would forgive him (the offender). He covered it so that another would not come, see and be disgusted by it, and not pardon the offender, with the result that the offender stumbles thereby. And it is good to follow this procedure.

"Whether it be good or whether it be evil" (Eccl. 12:14), this ending passage they interpret to mean one who gives charity to the poor publicly.[9] For this deed he stands in judgement because he embarasses the recipient. Also, one who gives charity to a woman privately, brings upon himself suspicion, for it is said, "Then ye shall be clear before the Lord and before Israel" (Num. 32:22). Moreover, he causes those who suspect him to stumble and be punished because of him, because those who suspect the innocent are flogged.[10] How do we know this? From Moses our teacher, who said, "But behold they will not believe me" (Exod. 4:1) immediately he became leprous.[11] Moreover others will not accept his reprimands, but will say to him, "You do such and such, and you are reproving us!" Therefore the supervisors of charity should not burden the poor man to work without pay, except for a meritorious deed, because the poor man fears them, moreover, he derives profit from them; also that the congregation should not suspect him (the supervisor) saying, "He (the supervisor) gives a greater portion to this one (poor man) than to the others so that he (poor man) should perform services for him," and the Torah says, "then ye shall be clear" (Num. 32:22).[12] "From every evil thing" (interpreting verse "whether it be evil" in Eccl. 12:14) refers to causative matters which a man causes deliberately, and inflicts pain on his neighbor, for this he is punished. Those who steal, take or conceal a thing which causes grief to the owner who must seek it, transgress a prohibitory law.[13] And so our scholars interpret,[14] "Ye shall not steal" (Lev. 19:11) in order to vex or to cause (another) pain. Even if he causes pain to an animal unnecessarily, by placing upon her an unreasonable load, and beating her so that she is unable to go, he comes under judgement for inflicting pain on a living creature.[15] Similarly those who pull the ears of cats to hear them shout are sinning. Our

47

scholars also expounded, "In that day Saith the Lord, I will smite every horse with bewilderment and his rider with madness" (Zech. 12:4). In the future the Holy One, blessed be He, will demand accounting from the riders for the harm they have inflicted on their horses for having struck them with greaves, which are called *eperon* in French.[16]

45. A man should always pray that no offense come because of him.[1] For instance the king Asa dug a pit [2] in Ramah; Ishmael, the son of Nethaniah, filled it with the slain.[3] Because he (Asa) sinned in relying upon Ben Hadad, the king of Aram, [4] this affair came about because of him, [5] (for the sages said) "good things are brought about through the agency of good men and evil through the wicked."[6] Go and learn from David, even though Scripture states, "He who comes to kill you, arise to kill first," [7] he did not want to kill Saul when he found him asleep in the encampment. He said, "If I kill him for my own benefit it will be a snare unto all Israel, for the nations will assemble and do battle with them (Israel). Better therefore that I be killed, and no stumbling come through me." And so we find with Mordecai, "And Mordecai stood not up nor moved for him" (Esther 5:9). He said, "If I stand up before him, the others will prostrate themselves to idolatry, better that they slay me and no offense come because of me."[8]

46. All your actions should be for the sake of heaven.[1] Let a man not eat nor sleep with the intention of being healthy and fattened in order to engage in matters of this world and to pursue wealth. He should rather say, "I will sleep and I will eat in order that I may be able to stand in fear of my Creator and engage in His Law and commandments." [2] And when he washes his hands and blesses, or if he recites a blessing over fruit, or a blessing involving any other deed, which is fluent in the mouths of all (a common prayer), let him direct his heart to bless in the name of his Creator who does wonderful kindnesses with him and gives him the fruits and bread to enjoy and enjoins upon him the commandments. Let him not act as one who does something because of habit and recites (blessings) without the heart's meditation. For this reason God's anger is kindled in His people and He sent us His servant Isaiah and said, "For as much as this people draw near, and with their mouth and with their

eyes do honor Me, but have removed their heart far from Me and their fear of Me is a commandment of men learned by rote" (Isa. 29:13). The Holy one, blessed be He, said to Isaiah, "Isaiah, see the works of My children, and know that it is all for appearances sake only. They hold fast to Me as a person who holds fast and follows the usage handed down to him from his father. They come into My house and pray in accord with the fixed prayers like the customs of their fathers but without a whole heart. They cleanse their hands and recite the blessing for the washing of the hands, they break bread and recite the blessing over the bread, they drink and bless (only) because the matter is fluent in their mouths, but at the time that they bless, their thoughts are not to bless Me." [3] It is for this reason that His wrath is kindled in Him and He swears by His great name to destroy the wisdom of His wise men who know Him and bless Him (only) out of custom but without devotion, as it is written thereafter, "Therefore, behold, I will again do a marvelous work among this people, even a marvelous work and a wonder and the wisdom of their wise men shall perish, and the prudence of their prudent men shall be hid" (Isa. 29:14). [4] Therefore our sages warned concerning this matter and said "And do things for the sake of their Doer (God). [5] For everything which the Holy One, blessed be He, created, He created for His glory. [6] Do not make of them a wreath with which to adorn yourself, [7] to boast of them when you perform the commandments before people. We will not reach the will of our Creator, because (as in the event mentioned) we labor to find favor in the eyes of men. The reward which we anticipate we lose, there will be none. He who performs secretly, merits greater reward, his deeds are ultimately revealed and he is exalted. [8] (The verse) "The end of the matter, all having been heard" (Eccl. 12:13) the Targum [9] Jonathan translates, "Everything that is done in this world will be made known in the future to all people."[10] It is reported of a certain man that he died prematurely. Long after twelve months he appeared in a dream to one of his relatives. His relative asked him, "How are you faring in the world where you are?" He said to him, "I am punished each day because I was not circumspect in reciting the blessing over the bread, the blessings for fruit and the "Grace" with wholehearted devotion, and they say to me, 'You intended only for your own profit.'"

He asked him, "Is it not true that there is judgement for the wicked only for twelve months,[11] and now more than twelve months are past and they are still punishing you?" He said to him, "They do not punish me as severly as during the first twelve months."[12]

47. "Who teacheth us more than the beasts of the earth, And maketh us wiser than the fowls of heaven" (Job 35:11). "Who teacheth us more than the beasts of the earth," (tells) a man to teach his son to be more faithful than a dog that is faithful to its master.[1] "And maketh us wiser than the fowls of the heaven," (this verse) tells a man to learn from the hoopoe, the hen of the prairie. Because, in the time of Solomon, it (hoopoe) did not fulfill its faithfulness to the ruler of the sea involving the "shamir" put in its charge, it choked itself.[2] Therefore let the remainder of Israel apply to itself the syllogism and take a lesson from the hoopoe which does not receive reward for guarding its faithfulness, or punishment for not safeguarding it. You, however, who are punished when you lie, is it not a matter of course, that you should not commit wrongdoing, speak lies, or let deceit be found in your mouth, one thing in your mouth another in your heart, but rather only truth, which is the seal of the Holy One, blessed be He.[3] And so did the sages say, "a just hin" (Lev. 19:36), your "yes" should be yes, and your "no" no.[4] The gestures of a person and the hintings should be just, also the movements of the head. When he bends his head and says "No" he moves his head to the sides, also let all his limbs be true.[5] (And so is it written) "Sincerely do they love thee" (Cant. 1:4). Rav Tavid said, "If they were to give me the vaulting of the world I should not change my words."[6] Anyone who varies from his word is regarded as if he worships idolatry,[7] for it is said, "And I shall seem to him as a mocker" (Gen. 27:12), and it is written, "They are vanity a work of delusion" (Jer. 10:15). And so is the punishment of liars, even when he speaks truth they do not listen to him.[8] But each one who speaks truth and does not speak or even think falsehood, his words are fulfilled, he decrees below and the Holy One, blessed be He, fulfills it from above. Concerning this it is said, "Thou shalt also decree a thing, and it shall be established unto thee" (Job 22:28).[9]

48. "He that is slow to anger is better than the mighty; and he that ruleth his spirit than he that taketh a city" (Prov. 16:32). Who is mighty is he who subdues his passion.[1] Be aware that man's might, strength and fear are all in the Holy One, blessed be He. And know that dissension, discord and the ear that desires to hear idle and vain talk and contentious matters, (all these things) bring the individual to anger. Anger brings one to sin, to serious transgression and forbidden matters, and one transgression causes another.[2] Do not exalt yourself over the poor man neither with your wisdom nor with your wealth for it is all vanity and a striving after wind.[3] Do not incline your ear to hear an evil thing lest you yourself stumble.

49. "And he said to him that did the wrong, 'Wherefore smitest thou thy fellow?'" (Exod. 2:13). He did not hit him, but nevertheless, with the raising of the hand he is called wicked.[1] Our sages said, "He who strikes his neighbor's jaw, is regarded as if he had struck the jaw of the Divine Glory." This means that he who strikes the jaw of an Israelite, as it is written, "And put a knife to thy throat" (Prov. 23:2), is regarded as if he had struck the Divine Glory.[2] He has no remedy but to cut off his hand, as it is written, "And the high arm is broken" (Job 38:15).[3] Therefore you, son of man, beware and guard your soul carefully, not to raise your hand against man or woman whether great or small, but only upon your son to reprove him.[4] And consider this in your heart: in the case of the man who marries two women and transgresses the Ordinance of Rabbi Gershom, the whole world says concerning him, "How impudent is that man, he is worthy to be banished and excommunicated," all the more so does that person transgress who strikes his neighbor or raises his hand against another, even though the person is not yet thirteen years of age.[6]

50. "The righteous eateth to the satisfying of his desire; but the belly of the wicked shall want" (Prov. 13:22). As the wise man is known through his wisdom and understanding and is thus distinguished from the rest of the people, so should he be recognized by his deeds, eating, drinking, sexual intercourse, toilet habits, gait, words and dealings.[1] And let all of these activities be most becoming and orderly.[2] Let him not be a glutton, but eat those foods suited for him to keep his body healthy. Let him not eat heavily, or be bent upon filling his

stomach, like those who gorge their stomachs with food and drink to the point that their body and stomachs are about to burst. Concerning them it is said in the Bible, "And will spread dung upon your faces even the dung of your sacrifices" (Mal. 2:3). These are the people who eat and drink and make all their days as holidays [3] and say to each other, "Let us eat and drink to the utmost for tomorrow we die" (Isa. 22:13). This (aforementioned) is the food of the wicked and their tables, the very same that he shamed. [4] Concerning them Scripture says, "For all tables are full of filthy vomit and no place is clean." (Isa. 28:8). [5] But the wise man eats only a dish or two and eats only to maintain himself, and not until his belly is full with all that the palate desires like a dog or an ass. A man should not leave less than one-quarter of his stomach empty. [6] And while eating and drinking he should not think, "I will eat and drink so that my limbs will be whole and strong." And during coitus let him not think, "I will indulge so as to have many children who will engage in work and labor for my needs." This is not the good way, rather let him take it upon himself to drink, be happy with his lot, keep his body healthy and his soul upright so that he may know God. For it is impossible to become wise in learning while he is sick or aches in one of his limbs. And when he has a son let him engage in teaching him, perhaps he will become a scholar in Israel. He who treads this path all his life serves God constantly even in the hour of everyday activity. And this is what Solomon said, "In all thy ways acknowledge him" (Prov. 3:6) and this is a small portion upon which all essential parts of the Law are dependent. [7]

51. One is forbidden to engage in slippery and deceptive words, nor should he speak with one thing on his tongue and another in the heart. [1] Rather let his insides be one with his word and that in his heart be that in his mouth. [2] It is forbidden to deceive people including the gentile. [3] And those who insult gentiles during an exchange of greetings while the gentile thinks that he means well, are sinners, for there is no greater deception than this. [4] One should avoid greeting the wicked in every way possible, [5] but in the interest of peaceful relations we can initially extend greetings to the more important among them. [6] Also he need not repeat the greeting, [7] for such is the custom that he who responds repeats the greeting twice. [8] And so one

should not prod his neighbor and say to him, "Eat," when he knows he will not eat.[9] He should not overdo his hospitality if he knows that the other is not receptive. And so let him not open (wine) barrels (supposedly in honor of his friend), that he would ordinarily need to open,[10] for this is to deceive, since it leads him (the friend) to believe that he opens them in his honor. Rather let him say, "Know that I do not do this because of you."[11] And so everything that is similar to this, even one word of guile or deception is prohibited, only let there be truthful language, a proper spirit and a heart cleansed of all perversion and vanity. All facets of a person should be truthful. He should not be contentious, scornful or jesting, for jesting and light-headedness bring a man to lewdness,[12] therefore let him not be excessive in laughter[13] nor sad or mournful,[14] but receive each man with a cheerful countenance.[15] Therefore he should not be a greedy person, driving for wealth,[16] nor lazy or shirking, but possessed of a generous eye, engaged in a little trade and occupying himself in Torah, and in that little (small share) which is his portion let him rejoice.[17] Let him not be quarrelsome, jealous, lustful or a pursuer of honor; for jealousy, lust and ambition carry man away from this world.[18]

52. The rule of the matter is let a man pursue the golden mean of each and every idea[1] until his thoughts are directed toward that mean. This is what Solomon said, "And let all thy ways be established" (Prov. 4:26). A man should not say, "because jealousy, lust and ambition are evil and cause man to be removed from the world I will try assiduously to remove myself from them (jealousy, lust and ambition) to the opposite extreme." And (if) he does so, so much so, that he does not eat meat, drink wine, reside in a suitable dwelling, or wear appropriate clothing, except sack cloth, hard wool and the like, as do Christian priests; (let him know) this too is an evil course and one is forbidden to pursue it[2] and must remove himself from it. He who treads this path is called "sinner"[3] because it is said concerning the Nazarite, "and make atonement for him for that he sinned by reason of the dead" (Num. 6:11), and our sages said, "If the Nazarite, who afflicts himself and abstains only from wine is called "sinner" and needs atonement, how much more so does he who denies himself all things.[4] Therefore our scholars commanded that a man should not deny himself (anything), except those things that the Torah alone

53

has denied him. Also he should not forbid himself through oaths and vows matters that are permissable. In addition our sages of blessed memory said, "Are those matters which the Torah already prohibited insufficient that you deny yourself other things as well." Included among these (people) are those that fast continually,[5] they are not in the good path, and so they said, "He who afflicts himself with fasts is called sinner, for he might be forced to rely on people." [6] But a person whose evil inclination overwhelms him is permitted to afflict himself and subdue his desire. Scribes, teachers, laborers are not permitted to afflict themselves so that they do not diminish their work.[7] For if the Holy One, blessed be He, desired fasts He would have commanded Israel.[8] However, He asked only that they subdue themselves and fear Him, for it is written, "and God hath so made it that men should fear before Him" (Eccl. 3:14).

53. "For line by line" (Isa. 28:10), the Holy One, blessed be He, may His name and His fame be blessed, recompenses measure for measure,[1] both reward for good and punishment for evil. How so? A man sins because of monetary matters, or because of his honor, or physical pleasures, woe to the sinner, for they (heavenly powers) will punish him for the sin that he commits. Similarly, if he merits and remains unconcerned with the pleasures of his body, wealth, or honor, they (heavenly powers) reward him with the very matter which he foregoes. For the king Solomon did not ask for his own perfection either in matters of wealth or ambition, but only in wisdom and understanding, to do his Creator's will,[2] and the Holy One, blessed be He, gave him both, even that for which he did not ask. Behold, everyone who does the will of the Creator and is unconcerned with personal advancement, profit or ambition, at that time when he is able to engage in his own advancement, the Holy One, blessed be He, provides for him.[3] Go and learn from Moses our teacher to whom the Holy One, blessed be He, said, "Now therefore let Me alone, that My wrath may wax hot against them, and that I may consume them and I will make of thee a great nation" (Exod. 32:10). But Moses showed no interest except to rescue Israel, therefore was fulfilled "but the sons of Rehabiah were very many" (I Chron. 23:17) and exceeded the 600,000 souls.[4] Therefore they established first the blessings "Favorest . . . with knowledge" and "Cause us to return," and "Forgive us,"

which reflect the will of the Holy One, blessed be He. It is written in Psalms, "but as for Me when they were sick My clothing was sack cloth" etc. . . . (Ps. 35:13) all are commanded to join in the grief of another,[5] to be troubled in his distress and to pray for him, as it is written, "far be it from me that I should sin against the Lord in ceasing to pray for you" (I Sam. 12:23). It is written, "Behold, He putteth no trust in his servants" (Job 4:11). Moses said, "all the difficult matters let them bring to me" (Deut. 1:17). He was punished for this in that he did not know how to answer the daughters of Zelophehad.[6] Samuel also said, "I am the seer," (I Sam. 9:19) and he was punished when he annointed David as king, not knowing which one he was of the seven sons of Jesse.[7] And so let a man not pride himself because people praise him, for if they do praise him, of what benefit is it to man who is here today and tomorrow in the grave, today alive and tomorrow a worm.[8] Of all the virtues humility is the most praiseworthy,[9] and so he says, "Now the man Moses was very meek" (Num. 12:3). Let a man not bear himself haughtily, or with a bare head for the Divine Glory is above his head, therefore he should go bent that His fear be upon him. Everyone who goes with a proud carriage, is regarded as robbing the Lord, rebuffing Him, and show-ing no reverence.[10] Neither let him walk with arrogance because of the fear of the Divine Glory which is opposite him. Take a lesson from those who guard a king of flesh and blood or one of his chamberlains, he does not raise his eyes because of fear of the king or the chamber-lain who is before him; all the more we who stand before the Divine Glory which is constantly before us, should not lift up our eyes. Rather (let) this be the custom, (let one) lower the eyelids to the extent that he does not see what is coming against the orb of his eyes, in French, *brunelsh*.[11] Meekness instills favor and reverence when a man lowers his eyes and bearing and does not go with a bare head because of reverence for the Shekhina.[12] Therefore let him always regard (re-member) his Creator as being before him.

54. What sort of murder is it that is not observed by the eye yet the punishment for it is very great, the transgression is light but regarded as very serious in heaven. It is "shame" and (this) refers to one who puts his neighbor to shame publicly [1] or causes him to suffer in the presence of another before whom he is pained with

embarrassment. It is as though he murdered him, because the other would surely suffer death rather than be so humiliated. One who shames his neighbor but later grieves and repents and is willing to receive punishment and comes before one who is God-fearing to find a way to repent, let them say to him, "Know that your evil is great, that you shed the blood of your neighbor." For so we find with Abijam, the son of Rehoboam, who reproved Jeroboam and shamed him publicly and was stricken dead.[2] Therefore go my son and entreat your neighbor until he is pacified, be exceedingly careful for your soul that you neither shame nor insult anyone. For the manner of penitents is to be exceedingly humble,[3] meek and submissively forebearing. And the meek do not retaliate insult for insult, nor do they reply. They are joyful in the afflictions of their meekness. And if fools shame you saying, "Remember your former deeds," say to them, "I know that I sinned greatly and I did many things unbecoming, but the Lord will forgive me." Endure those that shame you measure for measure, (if you insult them and then they insult you) for in this way will you expiate for your sins.[4] If his sin, involving unchastity, was made known to the public, because of this shame[5] let him not refrain from studying those laws that deal with unchastity. For it is better for him to obtain forgiveness in this world[6] since shame sheds blood and turns back perversity. And so we find in the Jerusalem Talmud, a murderer who comes to a city and is shown honors must confess, "I am a murderer,"[7] for it is said in Scripture, "and this is the case of the man slayer" (Deut. 19:4) this refers to "speech," that he verbalize and confess the slaying.

55. The penitent foregoes retaliation in order that his sins be forgiven.[1] For it is said, "Who is a God like unto Thee that pardoneth the iniquity and passeth by the transgression" (Mic. 7:18). He who is despised by men not because of his evil deeds, is destined to be exalted, as it is written, "Behold my servant shall prosper he shall be exalted and lifted up and shall be very high etc. . . ." (Isa. 52:13). And who is this? It is the one about whom it is written in a later passage, "He was despised and forsaken of men" (Isa. 53:2). "Every one that is proud in heart is an abomination to the Lord" (Prov. 16:5).[2] The man who is despised and loathed how does he dare exalt himself? Is he then iron, is his flesh brass? His flesh is but worm.

Even during his lifetime there are lice in his head and flesh, how then dare his heart become exalted. It is therefore best for him, if his strength be good, that he bring low his pride and haughtiness, if not, let him remember the day of death.[3]

56. "And that thou bring the poor that are cast out to thy house" (Isa. 8:57). More important is the reception of guests than to receive the presence of the Divine Glory,[1] for it is said, "and said, etc. . . . 'My Lord, pass not away, I pray Thee, from Thy servant'" (Gen. 18:3). Abraham said before the Holy One, blessed be He, "wait for me until I welcome the guests into my home." And a man is not required to give meat and wine to drink except according to his means.[2] His bread and water let him give with joy. Far better is a meal of greens with a joyful countenance, than a fatted ox with an angry face. At mealtime let him say to him,[3] "My Lord, eat with joy, drink your wine with a glad heart, for the Lord knows that willingly and with an eager spirit I would give you meat, but by my life, I have not what to give you." Concerning this it is said, "And if thou draw out thy soul to the hungry" (Isa. 58:10).[4] In the morning when he departs give him some bread.[5] Because of the fact that Jonathan did not give bread to David when he departed from him, it developed that the inhabitants of Nob, city of the priests, were slain, and Saul and Jonathan were punished.[6] Concerning this it is said, "For a man will transgress for a piece of bread" (Prov. 28:21). And as it is meritorious to be hospitable to the wayfarer, so is it meritorious to accompany them,[7] as it is written, "And Abraham went with them to bring them on the way" (Gen. 18:16). Come and see how important it is to feed the wayfarer. (Although) Micah made the idol and placed it so close to the Tabernacle that the smoke of the idol mingled with the smoke of the woodpile on the altar in the Tabernacle, yet the Holy One, blessed be He, said (concerning Micah) "Let him be, because his bread is available to wayfarers."[8]

57. "Bless the Lord, O my soul; and all that is within me, bless His holy name" (Ps. 103:1). The insides of a man, even his intestines need to bless the Lord.[1] Therefore he must examine himself well when he sets to pray,[2] because it is not fit to bless Him while bringing a belly filled with excrement before the Holy One, blessed be He. He needs to shake his entire body during prayer, as it is written, "All

mine bones shall sing, Lord, Who is like unto Thee" (Ps. 35:10).
It is written, "Guard thy foot when thou goest to the house of God"
(Eccl. 4:17), that your feet be not soiled.[4] And it is written "prepare
to meet thy God O Israel" (Amos 4:12).[5] When a man appears before
a king of flesh and blood he does not come attired as he would for
the street, he covers himself, and stands before him with awe, fear
and dignity; we who go before the Lord of all the earth, blessed be
His name, all the more do we need to cover ourselves and stand
before Him with awe and fear.[6] Woe to those who delay covering
themselves but from Sabbath to Sabbath so that people not laugh
at them.[7] They do not consider that perhaps they might die and be
unable to give honor to Him who gave His own garment, concerning
which it is written, "His raiment was as white snow" (Dan. 7:9).
Concerning these people and those similar to them it is said, the
wicked may prepare it but the righteous shall put it on. (Job 27:17)

58. "I will wash my hands in innocency"(Ps. 26:6). He who prays
must wash his hands with water[1] and recite the blessing for the washing
of the hands (one opinion) on account of the vessel which is called
antil[2] in the language of our scholars; (another opinion) because he
must raise his hands after the washing, corresponding to the expression
"and he bore them and he carried them" (Isa. 3:69). And in the same
manner that he must wash his hands for prayer so must he wash his
hands to eat bread,[3] but not so for fruit.[4] He must dry them well.
But he who eats without drying is regarded as if eating unclean bread.[5]
It is prohibited to treat the washing of the hands lightly[6] but he washes
with plenty of water thoroughly.[7] And everyone who is circumspect is
immediately rewarded in that he becomes rich like Rabbi Hisda, for
Rabbi Hisda said, "I carry a full hand of water and it gives me a full
hand of good."[8] Both for urinating and defecating one recites the
blessing "on the washing of the hands"[9] and "who created." He who
has just defecated or urinated and wishes to eat must wash twice.
He does not discharge his obligation with one washing, for the recital
of the blessing "who created" is an interruption constituting a diversion
of attention. And he who cleanses his hands with pebbles or rakings
recites the blessing "on the 'cleansing' of the hands."[10] In order to
eat, he cannot do otherwise but wash them in water.[11] Everything that
is considered as interposing in the case of "immersion," interposes
in the washing of the hands.[12] It is fitting that he have coarse flour

on hand in a vessel so that if he touches fat or blood or any other prohibited matter, he can remove all the dirt immediately, with the flour, otherwise if he touches any vessel or food it might adhere and he will eat it.[13] A man should not allow his nails to grow long lest mud gather (in them) and the scholars said, "Mud and dough beneath the nails, even against the flesh, interpose in washing,[14] moreover, tallow or prohibited matter might enter therein and lead him to sin." It happened that one saw in a dream a deceased righteous man and his face was pale, he said to him, "Why is your face pale?" and he replied, "Because my fingernails were long and tallow entered beneath them and I ate warm things without cleaning my fingernails,[15] also I would speak between the prayer, "and the heaven and the earth were finished," and the blessings of *Ovos* and *Kaddish*.[16] It is therefore advisable to pare the fingernails each Sabbath Eve. He who eats and his hands are soiled from eating, and wishes to drink wine, let him wipe his hands and bless the wine and drink, for it is said, "Lift up your hands to the sanctuary, And bless ye the Lord" (Ps. 134:2).

59. "For there is no enchantment with Jacob" (Num. 23:23). Our Creator commanded us, "neither shall ye practice divination" (Lev. 19:26). With our wrongs that are multiplied as of this day, they are divining in Israel.[1] They search their perversions and recall at the conclusion of the Sabbath not to eat eggs, nor take fire twice[2] if someone is sick in the house or gave birth within nine days, and many such things that the mouth cannot speak of wherein they transgress the commands of our King. And there is another form of divination quite prevalently practised. Standing and looking into the fire and seeing burning coals, they say, "We will have a guest,[3] however, if you extinguish it with water the guest will fall into the water," and there is no divination graver than this. And the contention that this is true and firm and that numerous people have proven it, is but Satan's doing, it is he who leads them astray. When Satan sees this one divining, and saying, "The guest will fall into the water," then Satan says, "I will go and throw the guest into the water in order to deceive him that this be a sign to him to divine for ever."[4] And woe unto those who do so, for they transgress numerous prohibitions such as, "Neither shall ye practice divination" (Lev. 19:26).[5] "There shall not be found among you etc.... . one that useth divination" (Deut.

18:10). "Neither shall ye walk in their statutes" (Lev. 18:3). More-over, they render false the testimony of the Torah, "For there is no enchantment with Jacob" (Num. 23:23). Those who vow when a headache occurs never to eat from the head of an animal, or when they suffer with their intestines never to eat intestines, follow the customs of the Amorite.[6] Trust only in the Holy One, blessed be He, and He will cure you. Also we need not be apprehensive about a sign, except in the way our scholars intended (directed us) as in the case where they said, "On New Year's let them eat of the head of a ram, because of the thought, 'Let it be the *head* of a good year,' also of various sweets because of 'a sweet year,' 'let him raise a cock,' also let him 'kindle a light in the house that the wind does not extinguish.'"[7] Those people that need to fulfill a command such as start the studies of their children, or some such other command, but say, "let us wait until the new month," even though this is not divining it is not good, for who knows whether he will live or die within the month, with the result that he may die and not fulfill the command. The best pro-cedure is to perform a meritorious deed when it presents itself and not postpone it, thus our scholars expounded,[8] "And ye shall observe the feast of unleavened bread" (Exod. 12:17). Do not say *matzos,* unleavened bread, but *mitzvos,* commandments, which is to say, if a meritorious deed presents itself to you, do not allow it to become sour but perform it immediately.[9] And if he intended to perform a meritorious deed but was accidentally prevented from doing so Scrip-ture credits him as if he had performed[10] it, for it is said, "And that thought upon His name" (Mal. 3:16). The Holy One, blessed be He, equates a good thought with action.

60. It is written at the end of Hosea, "Return, O Israel, unto the Lord thy God" (Hos. 14:2). Repentance is great in that it reaches the Throne of Glory for it is said, "Unto the Lord."[1] And it is one of those matters that had preceded the creation of the world.[2] It is equal in importance to all the sacrifices for it is said, "The sacrifices of God are a broken spirit" (Ps. 51:19). It does not say "sacrifice" but "sac-rifices of."[3] Let it not seem to the penitent that he is distant from the station of the righteous because of his past perversions, sins and rebellion, for the matter is not so. He is loved and desired by the Creator more than the righteous, for he has tasted sin and has sub-

dued his evil inclination and our scholars have said, "In the place where the penitent stand the completely righteous are unable to stand."[4]

61. It is written in Ecclesiastes, "Better is a handful of quietness, than both the hands full of labor and striving after wind" (Eccl. 4:6). It is of satisfaction to their Creator that "a full hand" is better, i.e., when a man gives to the poor and the God-fearing who declined in their wealth; "than both the hands full," i.e., to the poor that are not worthy but are filled with troublesomeness and bad spirit. Moreover, it is considered a sin on his part[1] if he gives to sinners, giving them the harlot's hire (and) strengthening the cause of rebels in the world against the Holy One, blessed be He. Therefore a man should always pray that the Holy One, blessed be He, prepare for him worthy people.[2] Another interpretation, "better is a handful of quiet" (is to give) charity with a good spirit and without anger, than "hands full" (of charity) which he gives grudgingly and with a bad heart, as it is written, "and thy heart shall not be grieved when thou givest unto him" (Deut. 15:10). Yet another interpretation, it is better for a man to support one person, if he has only enough to support one soul properly, than to give to five insufficiently. This results in "hands full of labor" because each one still lacks.[3] But if others are also contributing to each of these it is good for him to do likewise.[4] Concerning this it is said, "He hath scattered abroad, he hath given to the needy" (Ps. 12:9).[5] Even a poor man supported from charity must give to charity.[6] And each one according to his means, whether rich or poor, should feel himself beholden to the Holy One, blessed be He, in the sense of a *rentier* in the French, giving a penny, or (half-penny) half of this weekly (to charity).[7] This should be a fixed rule and without deviation,[8] to indicate that he is a servant of the Lord and that which he gives is a ransom for his soul.[9] Each penny adds to make up a great sum.[10] The poor man who cannot give a great deal, should perform meritorious deeds with his body. The communal leader is not permitted to force the poor to contribute to charity,[11] and he who does so is regarded as stealing (from them) for he steals from this one and gives to another.

62. "Happy is the man that feareth the Lord, that delighteth greatly in His commandments" (Ps. 112:1). Our rabbis expounded, happy is he who repents when he is a man,[1] that is to say, when he is in his youth and strength, when his passion seizes him and he overwhelms

it. "That delighteth greatly in His commands" and not in the reward for his commands. [2] And thus is it taught, "Be not as slaves who serve the master in order to receive fare and reward." [3] Let a man always think himself rewarded and put to his heart these thoughts, "if only in all my days I were able to correct the perversities which I committed. For everything that I do now, by right of justice there is no recompense, because all of my actions are useless, (not even) correctives to all my wrongs. O' that they could help me not to stand in judgement." [4] Even if he is thoroughly righteous and never did evil, yet by right of law he has no reward, for if he were to live two thousand years he would be unable to repay one kindness of even the very smallest favors that the Holy One, blessed be He, does for him.[5]

63. These things a man should ponder, let a man not serve his Creator in order to inherit the Garden of Eden,[1] but rather out of love for God and His commands, (knowing) that He created him and loves him. When a man is alone in seclusion let him reflect in this way [2] concerning those matters that are unbecoming. Were he before another person he would not act because of the disgrace, now too let him restrain himself. For it is the way of the wicked to perform their deeds clandestinely, saying, "Who sees us? Who will find us out?" And so did the scholar bless his students, "Let the fear of Heaven be upon you as the fear for one of flesh and blood."[3]

64. "Thou shalt not utter a false report" (Exod. 23:1). This is also a warning to those who listen to evil talk.[1] However, if a man comes to you complaining about his neighbor because his neighbor reproved him in your presence and for this reason he is angry with him and he says, "That one who dared to reprove, himself does such and such," and he continues to relate unpleasant things about him; if you know that after he tells you he will not go and tell others, because he does not care to inform the public, but tells you in order to unburden his heart, because it weighs upon him, it is a meritorious deed to listen to him. That which you are able to improve in making him beloved to his friend, do and arrange. Say to him, "so and so loves you, why then do you speak so?" [2] If he accepts, good, if not, even though you listened to his talk do not believe it. But you should not tell others in order to help him remove it from his heart.[3] For

others will be recipients of a false report and they will believe him. What will they do? They will relate to the other man the evil talk that this one spread about him, and he too will come to quarrel with him. The result is that the quarrel comes about through you because you did not listen to him. But if he tells others because he intends to spread an evil report about him, neither oblige nor listen to him. Rebuke him and dismiss him with anger. Go to them, to whom he had spoken and say, "Do not believe him, he speaks falsely about his neighbor." And when you speak about a man or woman don't relate the bad, tell about their good deeds. Do not praise a man in the presence of his enemy,[4] because he cannot bear to hear a good thing about him. As a result he will relate about him that which is shameful saying, "Why do you praise him because he did such and such, but did he not do such and such?"[5]Let him not praise a rich man before another rich man, nor a scribe before another scribe (similarly) or anyone who is in a like pursuit.[6] If he is God-fearing he may speak of him before another God-fearing person, [7]because the other rejoices in the fact that he is even more God-fearing. He is not envious of him but rather increases his wisdom saying, "I will do as he does."[8] And thus is it written, "Would that all the Lord's people were prophets" (Num. 11:29). Anyone who quarrels with a person and then tells about him something which he did not disclose before, do not believe him.[9] As a general rule, to all the matters which they speak of, do not give credence, merely act as if believing, but do not actually believe.[10] Similarly, a person who is profuse in the praise of his neighbor, but also benefits from this neighbor, do not believe him. Perhaps he speaks about him so because of the profit which the neighbor invites him to share. And so if you hear a man invoke God's name, for example, he wishes to relate what the Holy One, blessed be He, did for him for the good, namely such and such, do not jump and interrupt him. He may become silent in order to listen to your words and will speak no further about his matters. The result being that he recited the name of God in vain because of you.[11] But if he invokes it (God's name) to curse his neighbor it is meritorious to interrupt him so that he does not come to sin.[12]

65. "And his merit endureth forever" (Ps. 112:3). This refers to one who brings merit upon the community, for instance he teaches

the God-fearing the correct preparation of phylacteries [1] enabling them to assist others. If you brought merit upon the community and a transgression presented itself to you, but you mastered your desire and were rescued from it be not proud of it. Not because of the completeness of your heart were you rescued but God withheld you from sinning against Him because you brought merit on the community.[2]

66. An eclipse of the moon is a bad sign for the Jews [1] therefore he should fast, and inasmuch as one fasts because of a (bad) dream,[2] all the more so for the sake of all Israel [3] (as in case of eclipse).

67. "To punish also the righteous is not good" (Prov. 17:26). Anyone who punishes the public withholds the Messiah for if he were alive he would give birth. [1] Even though a scholar has the right to excommunicate where his honor is involved, [2] it is not worthy of a scholar to conduct himself so in this matter, rather let him close his ears to the talk of the illiterate. Thus did Solomon say in his wisdom, "Also take not heed of all the words that are spoken" (Eccl. 7:21). such was the manner of the pious of former years, they heard themselves reviled but did not reply, [3] moreover they forgave the reviler.[4] The great scholars prided themselves on their beautiful deeds and said that they never banished or excommunicated anyone because of their own honor. [5] Such is the manner of scholars, [6] who remain silent if spurned or shamed privately. But if degraded or shamed publicly, a scholar is prohibited to forego the honor due himself. [7] If he allowed it, he is punished because it is a disgrace to the Torah. Here he remains as vengeful and vindictive as a snake, until the offender seeks forgiveness from him. [8]

68. It is written, "Serve the Lord with gladness" (Ps. 100:2) [1] and "Serve the Lord with fear" (Ps. 2:11), but how so? [2] (both fear and gladness?) If a man is over-joyful, let him recall the day of death,[3] this is fear. If he is sad, let him rejoice his heart with matters of the Law, [4] as it is written, "The precepts of the Lord are right rejoicing the heart" (Ps. 19:9).

69. If you see a man of importance being spoken of frivolously, examine that characteristic (about which they speak) and you will find that he in turn has made light of some prominent person, or has stood by idly without protesting while that person had been scoffed. He is therefore punished measure for measure. [1]

70. Be well-liked by all people,[1] and do not pursue authority. Woe to authority for it buries its holders.[2] Proof of this is Joseph, who died before his brothers.[3] Do not become angered for anger leads to error. Go and learn from Moses, our teacher, who became angry with the soldiers and fell into error in that he did not instruct them in the cleansing of impure vessels that belonged to gentiles.[4]

71. One is forbidden to tear clothing or break vessels in anger, and one who breaks vessels in anger is called an apostate for this is the way of the evil inclination, today he says, "Do this" and on the morrow he says to you, "Worship idolatry" and the individual does so.[1]

72. "Therefore remove vexation from thy heart and put away evil from thy flesh" (Eccl. 11:10). And this is the best and most exalted of all the virtues. When you hear a man or woman say about you or against you something unfitting, put your fingers in your ears, for thus the scholars said, "Why are the fingers of a person shaped as pegs? So that if a person hears something which is not fitting let him place his finger or the lobe into his ear and not listen at all."[1] All the more, if you hear a man speak about his neighbor or a woman speak about her neighbor, where one cannot refute at all, since it is not your concern, shut your ears and do not listen as they revile each other. It is best for you to rule your own spirit and restrain yourself. Put a seal on your mouth without ever shaming your neighbor. Even if he relates about your father or your mother matters that are unbecoming do not answer unworthily, rather set his teeth on edge and say to him, "You do not tell the truth,"[2] and do not say another thing either great or small.

73. "But thou shalt fear thy God: I am the Lord" (Lev. 19:14). This is the great principle of the Law. Concerning matters which are dependent upon the heart, it is said, "Thou shalt fear thy God" Who recognizes your thoughts,[1] therefore let your thoughts be for the sake of heaven[2] and when you rejoice in your home rejoice for the sake of heaven. Do not become involved in another's quarrel, for what concern is it to you. And so did the sage say, "Do not express an opinion in a matter which is not your concern." For in favoring one you will be condemning the other, and in a person's absence,[3] you cannot act in his behalf to his disadvantage and so did Solomon say, "He who meddles in a quarrel not his own is like one who takes a passing dog by the ears" (Prov. 26:17).

74. Do not shame your brother when he speaks conceitedly of matters that the mind cannot grasp and it is easy for you to topple him from his arrogance and seize him in his words. Do not be eager to do so, for what will you profit in the matter? Do not chide any person, even a gentile, for long after you forget, he will continue to recall it as in the case of that individual who herded pigs.[1]

75. Do not raise your voice to answer arrogantly but all your words should be spoken with humility and dignity. For the words of the scholars are heard in quietness. Do not multiply idle matters.[1] If you stand among men, all the more so among women, do not speak excessively.[2] If scoffers suddenly come to your neighborhood and speak vain matters, do not reprove them lest they hate you. Leave them, for you might learn from their evil deeds, for scorning is second to immorality.[3]

76. Do not punish an Israelite, nor curse him[1] but pray for him that the Holy One, blessed be He, make his heart whole and return him to right conduct. Do not invoke judgement on him saying, "The Lord should avenge me from his hand and visit evil upon him according to his wickedness." For he who invokes divine judgement upon his neighbor, the attribute of justice comes before the Holy One, blessed be He, and says, "Lord of all the Universe, shall we then acquiesce to his request? he is deserving to be punished for such and such." The conclusion of the matter is do not curse anyone for very often all curses return and fall on one's own head and children, as in the case of David, we find that all the curses with which he maledicted Joab were fulfilled in his own children.[2] Do not hate your neighbor because of the love of your friend who hates him. One should not hate except him whom the Holy One, blessed be He, hates.[3] Moreover, it occurs at times that the two become reconciled. But he (whom you hate because of love for a friend) will not be reconciled with you because your animosity was without cause. Do not go about shaming people, for there is no man who is without his hour.[4]

77. Do not judge your neighbor with an inclination to his disfavor,[1] "For man looketh on the outward appearance but the Lord looketh on the heart" (I Sam. 16:7), and you do not know what is in his heart or mind. Be ready to judge all men in the scale of merit.[2] Guard your eyes from seeing evil and do righteousness according to your strength, whether that be more or less let one direct his heart

toward heaven. Submit to the Lord and consider in your heart that each man is the watchman of his servants, and all the more so that the Lord of the Universe will guard thee.[3]

78. Do not bring yourself to a light transgression for it will bring you to a more serious one. If one transgressed the injunction "Thou shalt not hate" he ultimately comes to the "spilling of blood (murder)," for it is said, "But if any man hate his neighbor and lie in wait for him and rise up against him and smite him mortally that he die" (Deut. 19:11).[1]

79. Guard yourself, do not sit with a man from whom you cannot learn good,[1] for woe unto him and woe unto his soul.[2] Moreover, you will cause others to suspect you of some evil matter, for they will say, "Not without cause did he go to him,"[3] and they will attribute to you all his evil deeds.

80. And if you inquire about a man with whom you wish to associate, ask who is his friend.[1] For a man does as his neighbor does. Therefore if you find yourself in a multitude, associate with the good person but not with the bad, lest you become evil as him. When you speak at night, lower your voice;[2] when you speak in the day time, look about you and be cautious in your words even because of the wall behind you.[3] For a man will die through the stumbling of his tongue but will not die through the stumbling of his feet. With the stumbling of his tongue he will remove his head but with the stumbling of his feet he will recuperate in a short time.[4]

81. If you are fearful of later regrets, say "no" before "yes." But to say "no" after having said "yes" is quite reprehensible. If you say "yes" twice, fulfill it.[1]

82. While you live seek repentance and do not delay, because death comes suddenly.[1] Do not speak at length without remembering the Lord to say "may it be His will," lest the heart become hard. And a hardened heart is one that is distant from God. Do not look at the sins of men who enjoy prolonged lives on this earth, saying, "their sins have long ago been forgotten."

83. "Be not hasty in thy spirit to be angry" (Eccl. 7:9). A pious man commanded his son at the time of his death, "As you respected me in my life so respect me after my death, fulfill my behest and let your anger rest one night and restrain yourself from speaking at all at a time of anger."

84. Let not your heart rejoice if they honor you, for according to the honor and pleasure that a person derives in this world from his deeds, they disallow from his merits in the world to come.[1] And should you say, "Did not Rabbi Simeon ben Gamaliel ordain that they should stand before him."[2] For the honor of heaven he did this, in order that they may be able to receive reward in taking upon themselves the fear of his office. Close your ears to the churl and the fool and look in hope to God. Do not laugh at a mistake of another for neither do you rule over the words of your mouth. Better that you keep silent and let him say shameful things about you than that you speak and call him sinner.[3] If he is an elderly man regard him as a child and do not answer him according to his foolishness, for he will then clasp his hands and choke.

85. If you did not prove your friend many times to be a faithful loved one, do not reveal to your friend[1] any matter that you conceal from your enemy, lest he change and become your enemy and reveal your secret. You should not reveal to any person the secret of another without his permission.[2]

86. The essence of wisdom is silence.[1] If a word is worth a sela, silence is worth two.[2] When I speak I regret, and if I do not speak I am not regretful. Until I have spoken I am ruler and master over my speech, but after I have spoken, the words master me.[3]

87. "And show thee mercy, and have compassion upon thee" (Deut. 13:18). He who has compassion for creatures, heaven will have compassion upon him.[1] If a person is not merciful there is no difference between him and an animal which is not sensitive to the suffering of its neighbor.

88. The wise man said,[1] "He who sows animosity will reap regret." The end of argument is regret, wait a bit and you will have no need to regret.[2] Scoffing dispels reverence.[3] It is second to transgression.[4] As our teachers of blessed memory expounded from Scriptures,[5] "All who scoff fall into Gehenna[6] and do not merit to receive Divine Glory." How shall a person take revenge of his enemy? Let him add new virtues to himself.[7] He who sets himself aright with the Creator, the Creator will set things right between him and others.[8]

89. Withdrawal from the world is leisure for the heart and rest for the body. Love of the world troubles the heart and fatigues the body.[1] And if people praise you for that which you do not possess,

worry.[2] Do not search out the secrets[3] of others and novelties, for these turn man's heart away from the Torah. Return fools, for repentance is acceptable and improve your actions while the possibility is still with you, before He comes in judgement upon us. For He is God, our Judge, whose eyes are open upon all the ways of men to reward each man according to his ways and the fruit of his doings.

90. You may obtain privilege in behalf of a person in his absence.[1] (And so) it happened with a certain person who constantly examined the prayer shawls in the House of Assembly, to see if they were torn or if the fringes had deteriorated. He inserted the fringes according to law and would then notify the owner of the prayer shawl.[2]

91. "But he honoreth them that fear the Lord" (Ps. 15:4). How so? For instance when he needs to show respect to his father and mother let him rise before them and honor them. After he rises let him return and sit down.[1] He does this even if he had in mind to go, for if he went it would then not appear that he rose to honor them.

92. A safeguard for piety is that the living should consider the accidents and misfortunes that overtake people and realize that because of their sins this happened to them. In the self-same matter wherein they planned evil they were punished, measure for measure.[1] As a result of this let a man examine his deeds lest it happen to him as it happened to them.

93. All Israelites are responsible for one another.[1] Were it not for this responsibility, no one would reprimand his neighbor for his sins nor would they care to search out those who do evil to eliminate them, but would only be concerned to make for themselves safeguards and fences that they should not sin. "Lo, all these things doth God work, twice, yea thrice, with a man" (Job 33:29). As soon as a person safeguards himself from transgression and overwhelms his evil inclination a second and a third time, thereafter the Holy One, blessed be He, guards him.[2]

94. "Though He slay me yet will I trust in Him" (Job 13:15). Let a man take to heart and take a lesson from the knights who go forth to war to show their strength at the behest of their lord. They do not flee from the sword, they are wounded and killed, all of this only because of shame; for it is regarded a disgrace if they flee. Moreover, dying in war they will not receive recompense from their

lords. Therefore, how much the more must we endure troubles and afflictions and make our peace with dying at the command of our King, Lord of all, blessed be His name.

95. A man should never seek from the Holy One, blessed be He, a thing that is unnatural.[1] For example, that his wife should give birth in eight months and the child should live or, (to pray) "May it be the Divine will—that I be now beyond the ocean! Even though the capability to do so is in the hand of the Holy One,[2] blessed be He, behold this is a vain prayer. One is forbidden to introduce into his prayer[3] an added benediction.[4] However, the rest of the day, if he wishes to recite songs and praises, may he be blessed.[5]

96. Let him not greet or return greetings to his teacher in the way that friends greet or return greetings to each other,[1] but he bows before his teacher with reverence and honor and says, "Peace be with you, my rabbi and teacher."[2]

97. It happened with a certain pious man who commanded his son not to enjoy this world more than necessary and that thirty days should not pass without a fast. When he died he was disinterred and flogged and people grieved deeply because of this. He appeared to an individual in a dream of night and said, "This befell me because I used to see tattered books with torn leaves and I did not assemble them and hide them."

98. Love to say "perhaps," and hate to say "so what."[1] This means, love to say "perhaps, if I say this thing," or "(perhaps) if I do," or "(perhaps) if I go to do or see this thing," or "(perhaps) if I hear this thing, or sweet songs," or "If I go for a stroll, perhaps it will cause me to sin." Let it be loathsome to you to say, "of what harm is it to tell of news and listen to vain matters as I please, I will not come to sin."

99. "Thou shalt not covet thy neighbor's wife" (Exod. 20:14). It is written without a *vav*,[1] do not cause yourself to be coveted. It is a warning not to beautify himself in order to find favor in the eyes of his neighbor's wife and instill his love and attractiveness in her heart. You should not appear desirable to your neighbor's wife. Another rendition, "Thou shalt not covet," one should not praise a pretty woman in the presence of his friend lest he pursue her and it will be his (the one who praised) sin. This is to say, you should not make the wife of your friend desirable to others. You should not de-

rive pleasure from the beauty of an unmarried woman, so much the more from a married woman in order that you may enjoy deriving pleasure from the splendor of the Shekhina.[2]

100. If unintentionally a meritorious deed came to your hand, rejoice and give praise and thanks to the Holy One, blessed be He, that He caused it to come to your hand for you to perform it.[1]

101. A man should not inscribe marginal notes in a book[1] because the book has sanctity and this has no sanctity. So much the more is it forbidden for him to comb his hair even over the blank area of the book.

102. It is forbidden to kill lice on a table at which you are eating.[1] And he who kills lice on it, is as if he killed on the altar, for the table is the altar,[2] as it is said "and he said unto me: 'This is the table that is before the Lord'" (Ezek. 41:22). And for this reason we cover knives during the grace, for it is said "For if thou lift up thy sword upon it, thou hast profaned it" (Exod. 20:25). It is forbidden to write in a book "so and so owes me so much and so much." "And round about Him it stormeth mightily" (Ps. 15:3). From this we learn that the Holy One, blessed be He, deals with the good strictly, even to a hair's breadth.[3] Because Sarah lied about Isaac, "Then Sarah denied, saying, etc. . . . " (Gen. 18:15) therefore the circumstance precipitating her death came through Isaac, for her soul took flight and she died when she heard the report of the binding of Isaac.[4]

103. Let a man always flee from miracles,[1] firstly, perhaps the miracle will not occur, moreover, if it does occur they deduct from his merits.[2] Greater is the merit of a handsome man who overwhelms his evil inclination more so than one who is not handsome, because he (the latter) is not acceptable to women.

104. Greater is the merit of a poor man who returns a lost object to its owners than a rich man (who returns a lost object).[1] The punishment of the rich man who does not return the lost object is more severe than that of the poor man. Merit corresponds to the sacrifice involved[2] and the goodness of the thought. If he thought to merit the multitude but is unable to do so because they do not listen to him, Scripture regards it as if he actually merited for them.[3] "For he that feareth God shall discharge himself of them all" (Eccl. 7:18).

71

105. Every commandment which has no seeker and no one to search her out, seek it, because it is as the deed of caring for the dead.[1] And a deed which has no pursuers, pursue after her to do it, for the meritorious deed says accusingly, "How inferior I am that I have been overlooked."[2]

106. A God-fearing man shall not reside in a place where people are suspect of (breaking) bans and vows. Each transgression is remedied by repentance, but when involving the ban and vow repentance will not cleanse him in this world.[1] It is, therefore, not good to reside with them for it is impossible that he should not derive profit from them or give profit to them. All who transgress the ban are regarded as if they transgressed the Five Books of the Law.[2] And if you count each word at the end of each book, "In Egypt," of the book of Genesis; "Their journies," of the book of Exodus; "Sinai," of the book of Leviticus; "Jericho," of the book Numbers; "Israel," of the book of Deuteronomy; and take the first letter and the last of each and every word they will total the word "ban"[3] and "ban" has the numerical value of 248, corresponding to the number of membrums in a person.[4]

107. He who prevents a scroll of law from being put into the Holy Ark, for example, he who protests in the synagogue before the ark,[1] similarly one who wishes to coerce and force the congregation to do his bidding and the leaders say "You act unlawfully," in the future the Torah will cry and call out over his soul, "So and so shall not come to such a place in peace."

108. And if you interrupt the prayer service and the leaders say that you act unlawfully and you do not listen to them, in the future they will pray, prostrate themselves, but you will not merit to be with them.

109. He who says to his friend, "Hand me a book" let him take it in his right hand and not in his left for the Torah was given with the right hand, as it is said (Deut. 33:2), "At His right hand was a fiery law unto them."[1]

110. To uncover the hair of a woman is regarded as indecency[1] and all that is said in the Song of Songs such as, "Your stomach a bundle of wheat, your thighs pillars of marble, your two breasts etc. . . ." all which is customarily covered is regarded as obscene to reveal. On the Sabbath let a man not speak about loved ones that died or are in pain, in order that he not grieve.[2] It is forbidden to

speak of idle matters on the Sabbath, as it is written "pursuing thy business nor speaking thereof" (Isa. 58:13). And so we find in the Jerusalem Talmud,[3] the mother of Rabbi Ishmael talked excessively, he said to her, "Mother, restrain yourself, because it is forbidden to talk." Rabbi Ami said, grudgingly they permitted greetings on the Sabbath, and only because the mouth is accustomed and conditioned to speak.[4]

111. He who is thirsty let him not bless and then pour off [1] but pour off first and then bless and drink; let him not drink and then give to his students, only if he poured off therefrom, lest the student be delicate and will not drink and die of thirst. [2]

112. If your friend sinned and you warned him, "Do not do so anymore and know that you will be punished," but he did not listen to you and transgressed, announce it then publicly, "I warned him and he did not listen to my warning."[1]

113. If the world speaks about such and such a righteous man upon whom there befell a misfortune, say to them, "He was seized because of the perversity of the generation,"[1] as it is said, "The breath of our nostrils, the annointed of the Lord, was taken in their pits" (Lam. 4:20).[2]

114. He who changes time honored customs [1] such as hymns and poetical insertions that all are accustomed to recite such as "God is unchanging" the poetical insert of the Kalir[2] which is the custom to recite, but he recited other poetical selections, he transgresses the injunctions "Remove not the ancient landmark, which thy fathers have set" (Prov. 22:28) and "Thou shalt not remove thy neighbors landmark, which they of old time have set" (Deut. 19:14).

115. If there is an excess of ink on a letter, let him not write God's name from it. Thus if excess accumulated on God's name, let him not write therefrom another letter.

116. "Love ye therefore the stranger" (Deut. 10:19). We are enjoined to love the individual who enters under the wings of the Divine Glory [1] in order to fulfill all the commandments of the Torah. In thirty-six places the Torah cautioned us concerning love for the proselyte, not to wrong them[2] either monetarily or through words. Greater is their love and more precious are they before God than His love for Israel.[3] It is a parable of two people, one man loves the king and the other, the king loves him. Who is worthier? Surely,

ness?"[1] How dare you not act, it will be held against you as a wrong and you will be punished. Go and learn from Saul who had pity on Agag and engaged in an erroneous syllogism, because of which he was banished.[2] And thus, "And a certain man of the sons of the prophets said unto his fellow by the word of the Lord, 'Smite me, I pray thee'" (I Kings 20:35). And through this he was punished, a lion struck him and killed him.[3]

127. A man should not eat or drink except if he be hungry or thirsty[1] nor delay his elimination even for an hour.[2] Inasmuch as a man needs to urinate or defecate let him do so immediately lest he put himself in danger of falling victim to dropsy.[3] The individual is obliged to keep himself healthy in order to serve his Creator and not transgress. Moreover, he would transgress the injunction, "Ye shall not make yourselves detestable" (Lev. 11:43).

128. It happened with Rabbi Jacob, son of Rabbi Yakar,[1] who would sweep (up) before the Holy Ark with his beard. And when the congregation went before the king or before the ruler then he would shod his sandals and say, "I am poor, they approach with money, but I with mercy and supplications, they with their means and I with mine," and so the congregation became accustomed to do after him.

129. "Honor the Lord with thy substance" (Prov. 3:9). You buy a box to safeguard your silver and gold, better that you buy a lovely box to safekeep your books and phylacteries. "Honor the Lord with thy substance," from that which He provides for your pleasure.[1] If you possess a sweet voice it is meritorious to lead in prayer. "This is my God and I will glorify Him" (Exod. 15:2). Make yourself pleasing to Him with deeds i.e., a beautiful citron (ethrog), a beautiful palm branch, a beautiful booth, a beautiful prayer shawl,[2] and so shall you do for all of God's requirements.

130. "Yet the righteous holdeth on his way" (Job 17:9). There is a man who is not sufficiently pure that God should accept his prayer. But because of the intensity of his supplications, the tears of his eyes[1] and his constant weeping and importations, even though he does not merit or possess good deeds, the Holy One, blessed be He, accepts his prayer and accedes to his request.[2]

131. If a man requests matters which redown to the praise of his Creator, such as the study of the Law or other matters of heavenly

discourse and pours out his soul for it, the Holy One, blessed be He, hears his prayer even though he does not possesss good deeds.

132. If a man asks your advice and you can advise, lead him in the upright way that appears in your eyes to be the will of God, but not according to his way which is against God's will. If you can advise do not remain silent, lest he ask another who will advise him improperly. Thus did it happen to Absalom when he asked advice of Ahithophel,[1] and then Hushai, the Archite, advised and he fell into the hands of David.

133. Don't take advice from one whom you suspect. He might advise you in a way he truly thinks best for you. Should you not succeed, it will result in your suspecting him and saying of him that for his own best interests he counselled badly and perhaps he is guiltless in the matter. It will then count against you as a sin that you suspected the innocent.[1]

134. The scholar said, "Give good and upright advice to all men who come to you to be advised, even your enemies." For two reasons, firstly, because of heavenly law, that there be no sin in you. Secondly, in this way you will exact revenge from your enemies. Inasmuch that your enemy thinks in his heart, "Surely this man hates me and did not advise me well," he will turn aside from your thoughts and do something else which will be to his detriment.[1]

135. "For this let everyone that is godly pray unto Thee in a time when Thou mayest be found" (Ps. 32:6). Our scholars expounded,[1] "In a time when Thou mayest be found" refers to a woman. He prays that the Holy One, blessed be He, should ordain for him a good wife, "But a prudent wife is from the Lord" (Prov. 19:14). The custom of the world is that a man follows after a woman, as it is said about Ahab, "Whom Jezebel, his wife, stirred up" (I Kings 21:25). It happened with a certain pious man who married a completely righteous woman but in time he gave her a divorce. He then went and married a wicked woman, a daughter of iniquity, and his former wife married a completely evil man. As a result, the pious man left his virtues and became transformed through the advice of his evil wife; the wicked man, through his wife, repented of his wickedness and became a completely pious man. Therefore every God-fearing man will not take advice from his wife involving the performance of commandments[2] because her eye is grudging, even if she is God-fearing.

wherein a person profits, whether from interest or his own hire or from anything which comes to a person profitably. If he found or they returned to him goods stolen from him,[2] he must tithe, as it is written in Scripture.[3] For Israel had not yet been among the nations of the world lending at interest.[4] Woe unto them that withhold their tithes, for ultimately nothing will remain in their hands but the poor man's tithe, as it is written, "And everyman's hallowed things shall be his" (Num. 5:10).[5]

145. "For anger resteth in the bosom of fools" (Eccl. 7:9). Anger is very bad and of necessity one must remove himself from it to the opposite extreme. Hourly, one must discipline himself not to be angered, even in matters where it is fitting to become angry.[1] If he wishes to cast awe upon his household or the congregation, if he be a leader of the community, let him appear angry before them but let his mind be settled upon him, as a person who shows anger outwardly but in his heart he is calm.[2] For anger leads to mistakes. Our scholars said, "He who angers, if he is a wise man, his wisdom departs from him." Men of anger, their lives are not lives,[3] moreover they die before their time,[4] and so he says "For anger killeth a foolish man" (Job 5:2). Therefore it is proper to withdraw from anger and to discipline oneself not to feel even those matters that anger him, and this is the good path. An ill-tempered man does not achieve but ill-temperedness,[5] and is drawn to say things unbecoming and even blasphemous.[6] Departing from anger leads him to the path of humility. Go and learn from Hillel, the Elder,[7] never had there been a person so humble as he, and his humility caused proselytes to come under the wing of Glory. Let a man not cast excessive fear upon his household lest his servants feed him forbidden foods.[8] There might arise an occasion when a dish is not quite ready, or some other matter, but out of fear his servants will go and serve him forbidden things and he will not know. He who casts excessive fear upon his household ultimately comes to three transgressions: incest, desecration of the Sabbath, and murder. Because of her fear for him, he will engage in coitus with his wife during menstruation or she will cook for him on the Sabbath. If he is accustomed to have a light kindled in his nightchamber before the Sabbath and she forgets to put it there, out of fear she will kindle it on the Sabbath. His wife or one of his children

may flee in the darkness of night and fall into a pit, behold, here is murder. Similarly, a leader of the community should implant fear in the community only for the sake of heaven.[9] If it be for personal benefit he should not dominate, oppress, and coerce them so that they fear him. How great is their (the leaders) punishment, for they are equated with infidels and apostates;[10] also informers who turn over their neighbor's money to gentiles, all the more so, those who deliver others bodily to gentiles; those who despise the scholars; those who deny the resurrection of the dead; those, who depart from the paths of the community; even though they do not sin, but are only separated from the community of Israel and do not participate with them in performing commandments; those who do not join them (Jews) in their troubles or in their fasts, not because of accident or illness, but because they go their way as gentiles of the land and as if they were not one of them; (also they) "Who caused their terror in the land of the living" (Ezek. 32:23), refers to those who put their fear upon the congregation not for the sake of heaven; they go down to the bottomless pit and never depart from there, Gehenna comes to an end, but their trials do not. For it is said, "And their form shall be for the nether-world" (Ps. 49:15), but fire issues from their bones and they are consumed.

146. If a person brings suspicion upon himself, let him forgive those who suspect him, since he is the cause.

147. "Thy statut have been my songs" (Ps. 119:54). David leaves all the songs and poetry of the world to engage in Torah. He reads the signs[1] with appropriate tastefulness, accentuation and song.[2] But those who recite the passages in the manner of scorners, mouthing them as ribald songs, in the future Torah will cry over them and say, "Lord of the Universe, your children make use of me as a lute[3] and at the time when they read from me with their arrogance, they do not read with the proper cantillation." Also those who interrupt the versification with talk, Torah complains of them, saying, "You have divided me into eight thousand five hundred sentences,[4] and they have divided me into more than six hundred thousand.[5] Moreover, they have done to me that which is not even done in everyday talk. A person speaking of secular matters does not jump from one topic to another but they interrupt my words to engage in banal conversation."

deeds), because they have said, "A man should always be deliberate (schooled) in the fear of the Lord."[1]Behold, one who has not learned, his heart is not like a sponge to absorb learning, and even if he has a teacher, behold, his heart is closed and at time disarrayed, he is unable to understand and know. And we find in the Torah that any one who is able to understand (what is proper to do) even though he was not commanded, is punished if he did not take the matter to heart.[2] For it is written, "And Moses was wroth with the officers of the host, the captains of thousand, and the captains of hundreds, who came from the service of the war. And Moses said unto them: 'Have ye saved all the women alive?'" (Num. 31:14). Why did they not answer him, "Why then did you not command us? You did not tell us to put the women to death." But Moses knew that there were wise men and experts able to argue a conclusion *a minori ad majus.*[3] If with the Caananites where it is written "Thou shalt save alive nothing that breatheth," "That they teach you not to do etc. . . ." (Deut. 20:16-18), and it is written, "For he will turn away thy son from following Me" (Deut. 7:4), lest he cause you to sin in the future, (they are to be put to death) these who have already sinned and caused others to sin is it not a matter of course that you should have argued a conclusion *a minori ad majus*[4](that they be put to death). Similarly, when the angels said to Balaam, "Wherefore hast thou smitten thine ass" (Num. 22:32), why did he not reply "What transgression is it that I hit my ass." Even the prohibition not to cause pain to a live thing does not apply. She did not buckle because of the load (but because of an angel that blocked the road). Also when she squeezed his leg why should he not hit her? Because he should have reflected, "Perhaps it is without the will of the Holy One, blessed be He, that I curse them. He permitted (me) only to reveal to them the future, for it is said, 'If the men are come to call thee' (Num. 22:20), you should tell them of the future." The Holy One, blessed be He, saw that he (Balaam) would rejoice if he were allowed to curse Israel, and this is what is said, "I have sinned for I know not that thou (angel) stoodest in the way against me" (Num. 22:34). (And yet) on the contrary the reverse stands to reason, because he did not know that he (the angel) stood opposite him he did not sin. However, he said thus, "I sinned because I did not take the pains to know, I did not examine and search into the roots of the (my) transgression." From this we learn that a man should be deliberate in the fear of the Lord since he is punished because of his ignorance. He must know and investigate, for in the presence of the Ruler you will not be able to plead inadvertence, as Shimei was unable to say to Solomon, "I forgot that I went out to the river Kidron."[5] It is for this reason that I said I will write a book for those that fear God lest they think that they are being punished without cause. Heaven forfend, attributing evil to God "For Thou art not a God that hath pleasure in wickedness" (Ps. 5:5), and it is written "Warn them from Me. When I say unto the wicked: O' wicked man thou shalt surely die, and thou dost not speak to warn the wicked from his way; that wicked man shall die in his iniquity, but his blood will I require at thy hand. Nevertheless, if thou warn . . . the righteous he shall surely live... but thou hast delivered thy soul" (Ezek. 33:7-9). The seven warnings correspond to the (seven) abominations of the heart: "There are six things that the Lord hateth, Yea seven which are an abomination unto Him" (Prov. 6:16); and to, "Seven times more for your sins" (Lev. 26:18). "But thou hast delivered thy soul" (Ezek. 33:9), mark that he does not say "thou hast 'merited'" or "vindicated" but rather, "thy soul hast thou 'delivered.'" From this we learn that anyone who has a friend that is being punished and he does not warn him and say to his friend "do not do so," all the punishment visited upon his friend is attributed to him as if he personally killed his friend, because he should have warned him but he did not.[6] Moreover, we exact from him the blood of his friend, concerning him it is said, "His blood will I require at thy hand" (Ezek. 33:8). For this reason have I prepared this Book of Reverence so that those who fear the word of God be circumspect. And furthermore my son be admonished,[7] (be forewarned) if I have been mistaken let the wise man set it aright and understand in order to fear God all of the days in truth.

154. It is meritorious to study the "forty categories of work minus one,"[1] so that he not forget which occupation is prohibited, in the same way that it is customary to expound on the activities of the festivals prior to the festival. So with the approaching Sabbath in order to facilitate the needs of the Sabbath, after the Sabbath eve service they ordained and instituted the recital of *Bameh Madlikin*,[2]

he receives for doing good.[13] Now that his evil inclination overwhelms
him and he subdues it because of the Holy One, blessed be He, he
receives the good reward. For those that are evil the good inclination
is bad, because if they did not taste the good inclination they would
have been able to say we did not know the value of the good inclination. If anything presents itself to you in accord with the will of the
Holy One, blessed be He, but because of shame you desist from doing
it and the matter seems awkward to you or if your evil inclination
overpowers you to transgress or to act,[14] reflect accordingly. If you
were living at a time of religious persecution, you would have been
visited by all afflictions, even death, for the sake of the Creator, for
it is said, "Therefore do the maidens love thee" (Cant. 1:3).[15] If they
wanted to kill you or inflict punishment upon you to the extent that
death would be preferable to life, you would endure them, all the more
in this matter which is not so great, where your evil inclination overpowers you. And the person that overwhelms his evil inclination
receives greater reward than for a hundred commandments where
his evil inclination did not incite, overwhelm or compel him to sin.
For they said, there is no reward for meritorious deeds that they
shall perform in the hereafter.[16]

"Before the evil days come" (Eccl. 12:1). These are the years of
old age[17] and the weariness of years of which you say, "I have no
pleasure in them" (Eccl. 12:1), which are the days of the Messiah
which have neither merit nor guilt. It is therefore better to do that
thing wherein the evil inclination overpowers him[18] but he subdues
his inclination because of the Creator, rather than commandments
wherein the evil inclination does not assert itself. You shall not say
behold the commandments are of equal weight, the light ones as
the more serious ones. He carries greater sin in a hundred commandments where the inclination does not bother him and he transgresses,
than in those commandments where the inclination opposes him.[19]
This is a parable to a king of flesh and blood who commands his
servants to go to a certain place. One comes and says to his (the
king's) servant, "do not go to that place where the king sends you,
and I will give you a pound of gold," the servant accepts and does
not go. The other does not go because one promises to give to him
two pennies. Behold this one accepts but two pennies his punish-

ment is greater, because he voids the will of the king in a small matter. Similarly, this one who sins in a matter where his evil inclination does not overpower him his punishment is greater. Anything that comes to your hand to do and you do not do because of the shame, lest they call you "pious fool," consider yourself as if living during time of religious persecution; you would (suffer death) over a light transgression even a shoestrap,[20](therefore say) all the more that I will subdue my passion which is given into my hand. If you stole learning it will suffice for you. And if the shame embarrasses you, behold it is for you as an atoning sacrifice.[22]Better that you be embarrassed before a hundred and not be embarrassed before tens of thousands after death.[23]And so he who withholds himself from a meritorious deed because of shame whether in a positive commandment or in a prohibitory commandment, he will be shamed publicly after his death in their presence and perhaps even in his lifetime, as with Zedekiah who said, "Lest they deliver me into their hand and they mock me" (Jer. 38:19), he did not submit to the Lord and they blinded him.[24]

Consider the two letters *kof kof,* "For every boot stamped . . ."[25] (Isa. 9:4) for the entire world is judged measure for measure for it is said, "because thou didst not serve the Lord thy God with joyfulness, and gladness of heart, by reason of the abundance of all things; therefore shalt thou serve thine enemy whom the Lord shall send against thee in hunger, and in thirst, and in nakedness, and in want of all things" (Deut. 28:47). And all who have mercy on the cruel show no mercy to the merciful. A man who is obliged to have mercy upon others, such as his sons, his daughters, his brother and his near ones, and they are in need and he is able to feed them but does not, behold everything that he possesses will come into the hands of others and he will receive for this neither merit nor credit.[26] Even if he supports others, but knows that his father, mother and brothers are poor and does not support them, in the end these others that he supports will deal cruelly and mercilessly with him; they will become his enemies and not consider it as a favor the kindness that he did with them. For there is a matter for which a person receives no merit if he does it, but if he does not do it, it is regarded as evil. For instance a man and his wife who love their children and they possess the means for their support and have mercy upon them, behold this

89

is no merit or righteousness[27]because out of love they do this for them, as in the case of dogs, bears and all animals who put their lives in danger to bring prey to their offspring.[28] If parents do not support their children or if they strike them unnecessarily or show no mercy to them or never admonish them and their offspring have nothing, the parent's transgression is grave. Therefore a father who does favors for some of his children and reviles others and does no good for them, him that he loathes will be his heir.

156. If you see three generations or more, one after the other, all scholars, but then their children are illiterate, do not say that the words of the scholars are voided because they said, "'Thy words shall not depart out of thy mouth, nor out of the mouth of thy seed, nor out of the mouth of thy seed's seed' (Isa. 59:21), thereafter Torah will no longer cease from among them." [1] Behold they have become wedded to a family whose destiny is not to have scholars in its midst,[2] and our rabbis said, "Most children resemble the mother's brother therefore their sons are illiterate." This likewise applies to the God-fearing and the pious, for it written, "and a threefold cord is not quickly broken" (Eccl. 4:12). And if you see that in the fourth generation the God-fearing and pious cease, it is then apparent that they intermarried with those to whom they were not suited, for instance he is not God-fearing or pious, therefore the generation is such. Therefore let a man seek favor each day for himself, his children and grandchildren, that they be joined to a partner who is God-fearing, possesses Torah and deeds of loving kindness,[3] for it is said concerning these three "and the threefold cord is not quickly broken." For the three words, Torah, fearing and loving kindness are all equal numerically, (fear is equal to Torah, and Torah is equal to loving kindness)[4] for concerning "fear" it is written "The fear of the Lord is the beginning of wisdom; a good understanding have all they that do thereafter" (Ps. 111:10). It is not said "to all who study"[5] but "all they that practice it," as it is written, "Oh that they had had such a heart as this always, to fear Me" (Deut. 5:26), and it is written, "What doth the Lord, thy God, require of thee but to fear the Lord thy God" (Deut. 10:12). Behold "fear" is prior to "all they that do thereafter" i.e., "The fear" of God and "love . . ." "to walk in all His ways" (Deut. 10:12). " A good understanding have all they that

do thereafter" (Ps. 111:10), "That ye may make all that ye do to prosper" (Deut. 29:8).

157. He who honors is honored,[1] he who honors the Holy One, blessed be He, and that which He commands, is honored by Him.[2] It is not proper that you put books on a bed which you slept upon lest there be semen on the bed or one broke wind in the bed, similarly it would not be proper that you hold between your legs or behind you holy writings, for it is said "And has cast Me behind they back" (I Kings 14:9). And it is not proper when a man has had intercourse in bed and the moisture of sperm is yet upon him that he mention any matter of holiness, prayer or Torah. Rather let him wash himself well with water that there not cleave to him even the smallest piece[3] (of semen). We find two purifications for three commands,[4] "The words of the Lord are pure words" (Ps. 12:7). "But words of pleasantness are pure" (Prov. 15:26). This is to teach you that a man should not be in a place of filth and think of matters of Torah or pray,[5] or speak to his friend of any matter concerning the Holy One, blessed be He, and neither (should he do so) when there is semen upon him. "The fear of the Lord is the beginning of knowledge, but the foolish despise wisdom and discipline" (Prov. 1:7). "For that they hated knowledge, and did not choose the fear of the Lord" (Prov. 1:29). "Then shalt thou understand the fear of the Lord, and find the knowledge of God" (Prov. 2:5).

158.[1] "The fear of the Lord is to hate evil, pride, arrogancy and the evil way, and the forward mouth, do I hate" (Prov. 8:13). "The fear of the Lord is the beginning of wisdom, and the knowledge of the All-holy is understanding" (Prov. 9:10). "The fear of the Lord prolongeth days, but the years of the wicked shall be shortened" (Prov. 10:27). "He that walketh in his uprightness feareth the Lord, but he that is perverse in his ways despiseth Him" (Prov. 14:2). "In the fear of the Lord a man hath strong confidence and his children shall have a place of refuge" (Prov. 14:26). "The fear of the Lord is a fountain of life, to depart from the snares of death" (Prov. 14:27). "Better is a little with fear of the Lord, than great treasure and turmoil therewith" (Prov. 5:16). "The fear of the Lord is the instruction of wisdom and before honor goeth humility" (Prov. 5:33).

"By mercy and truth iniquity is expiated and by the fear of the Lord men depart from evil" (Prov. 16:6). "The fear of the Lord tendeth to life and he that hath it shall abide satisfied, He shall not be visited with evil" (Prov. 19:23). "The reward of humility is the fear of the Lord, even riches, and honour, and life" (Prov. 22:4). "Let not thy heart envy sinners, but be in the fear of the Lord all the day" (Prov. 23:17). "Be not wise in thine own eyes; fear the Lord, and depart from evil" (Prov. 3:7). "My son, fear thou the Lord and the king, and meddle not with them that are given to change" (Prov. 24:21). "Grace is deceitful, and beauty is vain; but a woman that feareth the Lord, she shall be praised" (Prov. 31:30). Behold there are eighteen forms of "fear" corresponding to the eighteen forms of *Trefa*.[2] This is to say, even if they take the life of an individual let him not rebel against Him who gives life and sends death.[3] If you lose your life because of Him, He will resurrect you and if you remain alive in a situation where you are obliged (by law) to part with your life and be sanctified by His name, He will take your life, and who (none) will rescue you from His hand. And because life is dependent upon eighteen points in the body man is called "living"[4] for as long as there is no injury to them (eighteen points) he is able to live. Moreover, "eighteen fears" correspond to the eighteen points[5] upon which life is dependent, for if you fear the Holy One, blessed be He, He will guard your life and this is as it is said, "The fear of the Lord is a fountain of life, to depart from the snares of death" (Prov. 14:27). When Abraham wished to take the life of his son Isaac, he was then called God-fearing, for it is said, "for now I know that Thou art a God-fearing man, seeing thou hast not withheld thy son" (Gen. 22:12). The "eighteen fears" correspond to the Eighteen Benedictions of the Silent Prayer. And if you say, what of the verse, "A wise man feareth and departeth from evil but the fool behaveth overbearingly and is confident" (Prov. 14:16) where the blessing of the Lord does not occur, there is, however, the blessing against the heretics.[6] (And if you ask what of the verse) "Who so despiseth the word shall suffer thereby; But he that feareth the commandment shall be rewarded" (Prov. 13:13), (it is) in apposition to the first blessing of the Eighteen Benedictions which commences with "Blessed be He." Why are these "eighteen fears" made to correspond with the Eighteen Benedictions, for when a man prays, he must stand in fear,[7] for it is said "Serve the Lord with fear, And rejoice with trembling" (Ps.

2:11), and it is written "They shall fear Thee while the sun endureth" (Ps. 72:5), which our Rabbis explained (to mean) "pray at the setting of the sun." Moreover, why as against (in apposition to) "Fear of the Lord" does it state "Blessed is the Lord," (it is to say) that he should not run in prayer as if (to show) he is happy that he is finished. But with every word and everything that he says let him concentrate to put devotedness into his heart. One should consider, if there is a matter to entreat and ask for of a king of flesh and blood, would he favor you or countenance you if you hurry your words before him? Let alone would he not do your bidding, but he will say that you can mean only to mock, and he would drive you away. Do not regard the Crowner of kings less than the kings who are beneath Him. If you come to praise and adore Him, consider this for a moment, if you were to hear a sweet voice and song of praise rushed and hurried without intonation, how acceptable would it be? Therefore it (prayer) is not to be done hurriedly, but with deliberation and a sweet and loud voice, for it is said "And many shouted aloud for joy" (Ezra 3:12). It is said[9] that when they walked in the temple court they walked heel to toe so that the worship of the Lord not appear as a burden. Concerning this it is said "And their course is evil and their force is not right" (Jer. 23:10). Therefore the Holy One, blessed be He, created the cock's crowing that we learn a lesson from him, for it is said, "And maketh us wiser than the fowls of heaven" (Job 35:11). You would not be proper if you spoke before a king of flesh and blood, and your words were hurried, and if you sang for your pleasure you would prolong your voice, how then can you hurry before the supreme King of kings. You should therefore bless Him with your voice, and not make it as a chore that issues from your mouth. It is only right that when you utter words of supplication you say them in an entreating manner, for it is said "The poor useth entreaties" (Prov. 18:23). When a man entreats a ruler he does not hurry his words but on each matter he concentrates so as not to be mistaken with his words. Before he entreats a ruler or king he sets forth his petition orderly[10] that he not falter nor forget nor skip a letter. So should you do, for it is written, "Will thy riches avail, that are without stint" (Job 36:19), and he says further, "Take with you words" (Hos. 14:3). When you recite blessings and praises, make it as though you stand before a king and he says to you, "Let me hear your voice." Do not hurry your words and do not be anxious to speak. If you need sustenance, do not put your heart only to that blessing such as the blessing of "years."[11] If you have an illness do not set your heart only to the blessing for "illness,"[12] because they (will) say about you on high, "This individual imagines that he has need only of this."[13] Therefore let him (a person) be devoted in all the blessings. For behold the "eighteen fears of God" should be before him and he should be reverent of all the blessings. Do not direct your thoughts only to the supplications, for the essence of devotion is for the blessings and praises. They therefore said,[14] let him direct his heart toward all of them. If it is impossible let him direct himself to the blessing of *Ovos* or toward the blessing of "thanksgiving."[15] For if you direct yourself only to the (personal) entreaties there will be a hindrance from above,[16] it will be said that it is not proper to accept his prayer, for with the honor of the Lord he is not concerned to seek Him with devotedness and with supplication. How can we do his will if he is concerned only with his own welfare and not in adoration. Therefore it is good to pray and to direct oneself with joy and honor to the Holy One, blessed be He, to pray with devotion and not to speak to anyone before completing the service but recite those things that initially subdue the heart with mercy. And when you pray add in each and every blessing your request in keeping with the nature of the prayer [17] for they do best to prepare the heart. If you cannot add because the congregation already finished (the prayer), add in only one or two in order that you do not hurry in another blessing. You may add as we have outlined in the Order of Supplication.[18] If you cannot add, search out for yourself other melodies and when you pray recite them (the prayers) in that melody which is pleasing and sweet in your eyes, in that melody recite your prayers and recite your prayers with devotion and let your heart be drawn after that which comes out of your mouth. For a matter of request and entreaty select a melody which prepares the heart. For praise, a melody which rejoices the heart, in order that your mouth brims with love and joy for Him who sees your heart. And you are to praise Him with broad love and rejoicing. All of those things prepare the heart.

Lamed, why is this letter called *lamed?* Because of the verse "That thou mayest learn to fear the Lord thy God always".[19] (Deut. 14:23). For this reason David indicated with the letter *lamed* the teaching of fear "Come, ye children, harken unto me; I will teach you the fear of the Lord" (Ps. 34:12). Why does he say "children"? Because one who studies in childhood is not like one who learns in his old age. A son whose father led him in good deeds from his early years onward is like one who is accustomed to travel in a wilderness and is trained to find his way to the city. Similarly, he is like one who is accustomed to go by ship on the sea and knows how to direct the ship to the desired harbor. But he who does not know how to go, will go hither and yon, for it is said, "For he knoweth not how to go to the city" (Ecc. 10:15). And again, one who learns in his early years is likened to the sun, moon, stars, and zodiac, for they go in an upright path as it is said, "But they that love Him be as the sun when he goeth forth in his might" (Judg. 5:31). And this is as it is said, "But unto you that fear My name shall the sun of righteousness arise with healing in its wings" (Mal. 3:20). Therefore it is said, "Come, ye children, etc. . . . I will teach you the fear of the Lord" (Ps. 34:12). This is the teaching of the secret of fear. The letter *lamed* is larger than all the letters,[20] for the discipline of fear is greater than all, for it is said, "O, that they had such a part as this always, to fear Me etc. . . ." (Deut. 5:26). Behold before him is the greatest of all, therefore *lamed* is greater than all the letters and its name is greater than all and it is written, "Happy is the man that feareth the Lord, that delighteth greatly in His commandments" (Ps. 1:12).

159. "Wisdom hath builded her house, she hath hewn out her seven pillars" (Prov. 9:1). These seven passages in Scripture have coupled in them wisdom and reverence.[1] And these are them, "And the spirit of the Lord shall rest upon him, the spirit of wisdom and understanding, the spirit of counsel and might, the spirit of knowledge and of the fear of the Lord" (Isa. 11:2). "And the stability of thy times shall be a hoard of salvation—wisdom and knowledge, and the fear of the Lord which is His treasure" (Isa. 33:6). "The fear of the Lord is the beginning of wisdom, a good understanding have all they that do thereafter" (Ps. 111:10). "And unto man He said: 'Behold the fear of the Lord that is wisdom; and to depart

95

from evil is understanding'" (Job 28:28). "The fear of the Lord is the beginning of knowledge but the foolish despise wisdom and discipline" (Prov. 1:7). "The fear of the Lord is the beginning of wisdom, and the knowledge of the All-holy is understanding" (Prov. 9:10). "The fear of the Lord is the instruction of wisdom and before honor goeth humility" (Prov. 15:33). Behold there are seven passages relating to wisdom and reverence for the Lord corresponding to the seven matters that are evil for the soul and draw her to sins, for it is said, "There are six things which the Lord hateth, Yea, seven which are an abomination unto Him" (Prov. 6:16). Moreover, the seven correspond to seeing, hearing, speaking, working with one's hands, going on one's feet, cohabiting, plotting evil in one's heart. They also correspond to seven movements in man: standing on one foot; moving hands and feet; standing on knees; sitting and lying in four positions: i.e., on two sides (left and right), leaning on the head or on the face. Another interpretation of "seven organs," (is that it applies to) eyes, ears, a mouth to bring forth words, a throat to bring in food and drink, hands, feet, genitals, these are "She hath hewn out her seven pillars." "Hath builded her house" (Prov. 9:1), for all of them (organs) depend upon the chamber of the heart [2] which leads wisdom to contain and restrain his spirit in the fear of God. Concerning the seven transgressions wherein I wrote that the heart is their master, there are corresponding to them seven groups which receive the Divine Presence.[3]

160. If you were put to a test and you kept yourself from sinning, do not boast of it saying, "I withstood the test."[1] Perhaps your forefathers came to the same test and did not sin and they asked of the Holy One, blessed be He, that when their sons come to the same test they be given the power to keep from sinning,[2] for it is said, "God will provide Himself the lamb for a burnt offering my son etc. . . . and Abraham called the name of that place Adonaijireh"[3] (Gen. 22:8-15). His children will be slaughtered in Sanctification of the Name and burnt like Isaac.[4] You should bless the Holy One because he strengthened you over your inclination, and gave you a heart to be victorious over your evil inclination,[5] for it is said, "God left him to try him" (II Chron. 32:31). "Left him," from this it is apparent that all is in His hand. For this reason David en-

treated Him, for it is said, "Make one my heart to fear Thy name" (Ps. 86:11), and it is written, "And renew a steadfast spirit within me" (Ps. 51:12).

161. If you withstood a great test still do not be confident of yourself until the day of death,[1] to say, "Since I did not sin in this great matter, I will no longer sin." Because the evil inclination today is not the same as yesterday, therefore perhaps in the very same matter (test) tomorrow you will be unable to endure. Behold David did not sin with Abigail[2] but he sinned with Bathsheba, David did not sin with his pursuers who sought to kill him[3] and did not raise his hand upon the annointed of God and did not give permission to Avishai to strike him,[4] but in the end he did sin with Uriah, who sought his (David's) wellbeing.[5] But if you say, "I can believe in myself since I was rescued from a great transgression," then you hold yourself more righteous than those on high. Not only that, but you regard yourself and your wisdom superior to Him who created you, for it is said, "Behold, He putteth no trust in His holy ones" (Job 15:15), "And His angels He chargeth with folly" (Job 4:18). If the Holy One, blessed be He, who knows what the future will be, does not trust His angels and His holy ones, you, with your thoughts changing from good to evil all the more that you should not be confident in yourself, and thus it is said, "Happy is the man that feareth always" (Prov. 28:14) that he not sin. "Lamed," signifies "Your heart, fill it with understanding,"[6] to know the fear of the Lord, and it is written, "Teach me good discernment and knowledge . . . teach me Thy statutes" (Ps. 119:66-68).

FOOTNOTES

/1/ Gershom Scholem, *Major Trends in Jewish Mysticism* (New York: Schocken Books, 1946), p. 81.

/2/ *Ibid.*

/3/ Adolf Kober, *Cologne* (Philadelphia: Jewish Publication Society, 1940), p. 5.

/4/ Max Grunwald, *History of the Jews in Vienna* (Philadelphia: Jewish Publication Society, 1936), p. 1. See also, Cecil Roth, "Economic Life and Population Movements," *The World History of the Jewish People,* ed. Cecil Roth, XI (1966), 16: "Evidence shows the existence of a well organized Jewish community on the Rhineland in the early fourth century during the reign of Constantine."

/5/ B. Blumenkranz, "Germany 843-1096," *The World History of the Jewish People,* ed. Cecil Roth, XI (1966), 163. Also Grunwald, p. 41.

/6/ Salo W. Baron, *A Social and Religious History of the Jews* (8 Vols.; 2d ed. rev.; Philadelphia: Jewish Publication Society, 1958) IV, 90.

/7/ *Ibid.,* 132ff. One of the finest and most perceptive treatments of medieval millenary movements is Norman Cohn's, *The Pursuit of the Millenium* (New York: Harper and Brothers, 1961).

/8/ Roth, XI, 36-37.

/9/ Solomon Grayzel, *The Church and the Jews in the Thirteenth Century* (ed. rev.; New York: Herman Press, 1966), p. 306: "Volentes igitur in hac parte prospicere Christianis ne a Judeis immaniter aggraventur . . ." (IV Lateran Council—1215).

/10/ Sholom A. Singer, "The Expulsion of the Jews from England in 1290," *Jewish Quarterly Review,* LV (October 1964), 117ff.

/11/ Grayzel, p. 10.

/12/ Abraham Epstein, *Collected Writings* (2 Vols.; Jerusalem: Mosad Harav Kook, 1950), I. 250, note 10. A complete discussion is presented by the author concerning Judah's birthplace. The other ascribed birthplace, Worms, Epstein rejects. I. Elbogen, A. Freimann and R. Tykocinski in *Germania Judaica* (2d ed.; Breslau: Verlag M. and H. Marcus, 1934), p. 293, agree with Epstein in choosing Speyer as the birthplace. Interesting to note is Scholem's reference to Judah the Hasid of Worms (Scholem, p. 82).

/13/ V. Aptowitzer, *Introduction to Sefer Rabiah* (Jerusalem: Mekize Nirdamim, 1938), p. 348, note 20. The author presents convincing arguments in support of this rather than a later date. See also, J. Freimann in his introduction to *Sefer Hasidim,* Parma MS, Cod. de Rossi No. 1133, ed. Jacob Freimann and Jehuda Wistinetzki (2d ed.; Frankfort: M. A. Wahrmann Verlag, 1924), p. 14. Future reference to this will be designated as *S. H.,* Parma MS.

/14/ Baron, VIII, 42 (*ca.,* 1140-1217); also Scholem, p. 82; Aptowitzer, p. 344; and Epstein, I, 150.

/15/ Isaac Broyde, "Kalonymus," *Jewish Encyclopedia,* ed. Isidore Singer, VII (1904), 424a.

/16/ Epstein, I, 251. The author provides a complete genealogical chart of Samuel's forbears and descendants (Epstein, I, 248). This would have stabilized matters had it not been challenged by Aptowitzer, p. 348.

/17/ Scholem, p. 82.

/18/ Epstein, I, 260, ascribes the two chapters in *S. H.,* Parma MS, on "God-fearing" and "Repentance," sections 1 through 26, to Samuel He-Hasid.

/19/ Epstein, I, 250; Aptowitzer, p. 344; and Freimann in his introduction to *S. H.,* Parma MS, p. 3, have a rather strenuous go at the difficult problem of identifying Samuel the Pious' children. All three agree that he had two sons, one being Judah. They fail to agree on the identity of the other son. Aptowitzer further maintains that the person of Golda, usually described as Judah's sister, is in fact Judah's granddaughter.

/20/ Epstein makes mention of the fact that the *Ma'aseh Book,* trans. Moses Gaster (2 Vols.; Philadelphia: Jewish Publication Society, 1934), II, 326, records the name of Eleazer, supposedly a twin brother of Abraham. However he concludes quite plausibly and convincingly that the reference may be dismissed since it occurs just this one time and the source itself is not completely beyond question.

/21/ Epstein, I, 252.

/22/ *Ma'aseh Book,* II, 336.

/23/ Aptowitzer, p. 346, challenges the date 1195 or 1196 as the time when Judah arrived in Regensburg. Contrary to Epstein and Freimann, he pushes it back prior to 1175.

/24/ This point will be discussed at length in a special section.

/25/ Here again the problem of identifying, let alone numbering, the descendants properly becomes quite difficult. A good deal of controversy among scholars persists. See Freimann's remarks in his introduction to *S. H.,* Parma MS, pp. 2-3; Aptowitzer, p. 344; and Epstein, I, 248.

/26/ Freimann, *S. H.,* Parma MS, p. 2.

/27/ *Ibid.* The identification of this individual is quite difficult.

/28/ See *Ma'aseh Book* for much of the anecdotal material and legend on the life of Judah and many other notable rabbis.

/29/ *Germania Judaica,* p. 293.

/30/ Baer, "Religious Social Tendency of the Sefer Hasidim," *Zion,* III (1938), 1-50, cited by Scholem, p. 83.

/31/ This, I would say, is the general consensus among scholars and most widely accepted opinion. See Freimann, *S. H.,* Parma MS, p. 12.

/32/ M. Gudemann, quoted by *Jewish Encyclopedia,* VII, 357.

/33/ Freimann, *S. H.,* Parma MS, p. 10, gives a very succinct and useful presentation of the major points of view in this very dubious matter of authorship.

/34/ *Ibid.*

/35/ Epstein, I, 259.

/36/ Graetz is one such case. He ascribes the book to R. Judah ben Isaac of Paris (b. 1166-d. 1224) sometimes called Sir Leon. Graetz does this on the strength of the French expressions occurring in the text. See article on "Judah ben Samuel He-Hasid," *Jewish Encyclopedia,* VII, 357.

/37/ Baer, *Zion,* III, 1-50.

/38/ Examples abound in which conflicting directives are put forward.

/39/ Judah Rosenthal, "L'Toldoth Ha-Siddur," reprint from *Hadoar* (Shebat 5707), p. 11. This article helps us to appreciate more fully the rich resource of the prayer for investigating the diverse elements in the spiritual development of Judaism.

/40/ There is no complete unanimity on precisely who might be deemed a *hasid.* Very often terms other than *hasid* are used in a context designating piety. Often the attributes and qualities involved in piety are indicated without reference to an individual. It might be said, except in one instance of which I am aware, that the various scholars commenting and writing on this subject have used such excellent discretion and fair-mindedness in their handling of the references to "piety," *hasid,* etc., that the question of taking liberties with the meaning seldom arises. Needless to say, the temptation to give infinite elasticity and application to the term *hasid* so as to cover almost everything, is great.

/41/ Scholem, p. 92. See also, Norman M. Bronznick, "Some Aspects of German Jewish Mysticism as Reflected in the *Sefer Hasidim*" (unpublished M. A. dissertation, Department of Philosophy, Columbia University, 1947), p. 8, for a discussion of these categories and their component elements.

/42/ Judah the Pious, *Sefer Hasidim,* (Jerusalem: Mosad Harav Kook, 1957), secs. 7, 9, 10, 11. This version is generally referred to as the Bologna Edition. Future references will be designated as *S. H.,* Bologna Ed.

/43/ *Ibid.,* secs. 7, 10, 11.

/44/ *Ibid.,* secs. 7, 9, 10, 29.

/45/ *Ibid.,* secs. 10, 29.

/46/ *Ibid.,* secs. 9, 10, 12.

/47/ Baer, *Zion,* III, 12.

/48/ *S. H.,* Bologna Ed., sec. 44.

/49/ *Ibid.,* sec. 11.

/50/ See passages quoted in *S. H.,* Parma MS, sec. 975, p. 240, note 1.

/51/ *S. H.,* Bologna Ed., sec. 378, quotes statement from Kiddushin 21b.

/52/ Berliere is quoted by Ray C. Petry, *Late Medieval Mysticism,* Vol. XIII of *The Library of Christian Classics,* ed. John Baillie and others (Philadelphia: Westminster Press, 1953—), 19.

/53/ Evelyn Underhill, *Mysticism* (New York: E. P. Dutton and Co., 1960), p. 167. This is found in Platonic and Neoplatonic thought. In view of the long history of Judaism something of this is therefore to be anticipated in the Jewish mystic.

/54/ H. H. Ben-Sasson, *On Jewish History in the Middle Ages* (Tel Aviv: Am Oved Limited, 1958), p. 190. Briefly, the author touches upon parallels between the German pietists and the Franciscans and some of their common characteristics. Also see Baron, *Social and Religious History of the Jews,* VIII, 295, note 54.

/55/ Petry, *Late Medieval Mysticism,* 30: "In the balance of the contemplative and the active, there is in Augustine, as later in Gregory and Bernard, an incitement to Christian service and responsibility that inspired the whole of the Middle Ages."

/56/ *Ibid.,* 319, quoting Rysbroeck in *The Sparkling Stone,* Chapter XIV.

/57/ *Ibid.,* 207, quoting from *Love Can Not Be Lazy,* Meister Eckhart.

/58/ Ray C. Petry, "Social Responsibility and the Late Medieval Mystics," *Church History,* Vol. XXI (1952). Here he develops the theme of balanced contemplation and action for many of the medieval mystics.

/59/ Petry, *Late Medieval Mysticism,* 18.

/60/ Scholem, *Major Trends in Jewish Mysticism,* p. 91; Baer, *Zion,* III, 27.

/61/ First published in Bologna in 1538 by Abraham the son of Moses the Priest. Apparently published without censorship. See Freimann's introduction to *S. H.,* Parma MS, p. 9.

/62/ A publishing house in Israel specializing in Hebraica and Judaica texts.

/63/ Published by the Mekize Nirdamim Society during the years 1891 to 1893 based on MSS attributed to the thirteenth century. See Freimann's introduction to *S. H.,* Parma MS, p. 9.

/64/ Freimann's introduction to *S. H.,* Parma MS, p. 19. See also Epstein, I, 258, note 24, wherein he agrees with Freimann and offers additional evidence.

/65/ Freimann's introduction to *S. H.*, Parma MS, p. 19.

/66/ In the Mosad Rav Kook edition this unit forms an evenly rounded book in and of itself, secs. 1-161.

/67/ Where the transliteration varies from the Jewish Publication Society system, the alternate form can be found in either the Soncino edition of the Talmud or in Danby's English rendering of the Mishnah.

/68/ Exceptions to the Jewish Publication Society system of transliteration are h, t, k, and s, also the use of the apostrophe to indicate the Hebrew letter "Ayin," and the dieresis. These have been omitted because they are unnecessary for the Hebraist and meaningless to the non-Hebraist.

/69/ Ferreting out sources for many of the statements occurring in *Sefer Hasidim* would have been insurmountable if not for the spade-work done by Reuben Margulies in his commentary Mekor Hesed. It proved to be an invaluable aid. However, there is one word of caution, numerous citations found in Mekor Hesed are incorrect, many are unquestionably printers errors; wherever possible I have made the proper correction.

For an admirable study of the theology of *Haside Ashkenaz,* see Joseph Dan, *Torat Ha-Sod shel Hasidut Ashkenaz* (Jerusalem: Mosad Bialik, 1968).

TEXT

SEC. 3

/1/ Yoma 37a. All Talmudic references are to the Babylonian Talmud unless otherwise indicated.

/2/ *Ibid.,* 35b.

/3/ Kiddushin 31b.

/4/ Nedarim 7b.

SEC. 4

/1/ Megillah 3a.

SEC. 5

/1/ Arakhin 16b.

/2/ Shabbath 54b.

/3/ Baba Metzia 31a.

/4/ *Ibid.*

/5/ Berakoth 19b.

/6/ Baba Metzia 31b.

/7/ Sanhedrin 18a.

/8/ Shabbath 54b.

/9/ Arakhin 16b.

/10/ Shabbath 34a.

/11/ *Sifra,* ed. Isaac H. Weiss (reprint of Vienna Edition of 1862; New York: OM Publishing Co., 1947), p. 89a.

SEC. 6

/1/ Arakhin 15b.

/2/ Maimonides, Hilkhoth Deoth, 6:8.

SEC. 7

/1/ Baba Metzia 58b.

/2/ Berakoth 12b.

/3/ Shabbath 104a.

/4/ *Midrash Tehillim,* ed. Solomon Buber (Wilna: Romm Publisher, 1891), p. 313.

/5/ Aboth 4:2.

/6/ Samuel 16:7.

/7/ Hullin 94a.

/8/ Aboth 5:26.

––––––––

SEC. 8

/1/ *Aboth of Rabbi Nathan,* ed. Solomon Schechter (reprint of Vienna Edition of 1887; New York: P. Feldheim Publisher, 1945), version A, Chapter XXXVIII, p. 114.

/2/ *Yalkut Shimoni* (New York—Berlin: Horeb Publishers, 1926), Kings, par. 244, p. 768.

––––––––

SEC. 9

/1/ Ben Sira 9:5.

/2/ Baba Bathra 57b.

/3/ Berakoth 24a.

/4/ Solomon Ibn Gabirol, *Choice of Pearls,* ed. Zvi Phillipawski (Warsaw: J. Lebenson, 1863), p. 9; also Jerusalem Talmud Berakoth 1:5. All future references to the Jerusalem Talmud will be designated J. T.

––––––––

SEC. 10

/1/ The term *hasid* used to describe the pious and saintly, derives from the Hebrew word *hesed,* meaning act of loving kindness.

/2/ *Midrash Tehillim,* ed. Buber, p. 123.

/3/ *Midrash Rabbah* (New York-Berlin: Horeb Publishers, 1924), Leviticus, Chapter XXX, p. 81a.

––––––––

SEC. 12

/1/ *Sifra,* ed. Weiss, p. 93b.

––––––––

SEC. 13

/1/ Hagigah 10a.

/2/ Aboth 5:3.

/3/ Berakoth 17a.

/4/ *Ibid.*

/5/ *Ibid.*

/6/ Berakoth 6b.

/7/ Shabbath 31b.

SEC. 14

/1/ The term "love" is the preferred reading.

/2/ *Ibid.*

/3/ Berakoth 61b.

/4/ Nedarim 62a.

/5/ Rosh ha-Shanah 4a.

/6/ Shabbath 75a.

/7/ Maimonides, Hilkhoth Teshuvah, 10:6.

/8/ Moses Maimonides, *Book of the Divine Commandments,* trans. Charles Chavel (2 Vols.; London: Soncino Press, 1940), I, 82, commandment 3.

/9/ Maimonides, Hilkhoth Yesode Ha-Torah, 2:2, adds the words, "Who is omniscient," (literally, "Whose knowledge is complete").

SEC. 15

/1/ Rashi, Shabbath 30b.

/2/ *Mekilta,* ed. Jacob Z. Lauterbach (3 Vols.; Philadelphia: Jewish Publication Society, 1933-1935), Exodus II, 140.

/3/ Sanhedrin 11b.

/4/ Sanhedrin 38b.

/5/ Erubin 13b.

/6/ Let him show respect to others.

/7/ Aboth 1:17.

/8/ Aboth 5:10.

/9/ Gittin 56a.

/10/ Pesahim 100a.

/11/ Rashi, Ketuboth 69a.

/12/ Betzah 5b.

/13/ Sotah 22b.

/14/ Megillah 28a.

/15/ *Aboth of Rabbi Nathan,* ed. Schechter, version A, Chapter XXXIX, p. 87.

/16/ Berakoth 34a.

/17/ *Ibid.,* 55b.

/18/ Ketuboth 46a.

/19/ Hullin 44b.

/20/ Ketuboth 46a.

SEC. 16

/1/ Abodah Zarah 20a.

/2/ *Ibid.*

/3/ *Ibid.*

/4/ Sotah 8b.

/5/ J. T. Pesahim 6:1.

SEC. 17

/1/ Nedarim 62a.

/2/ *Sifra,* ed. Weiss, p. 110b; also Taanith 7a.

/3/ Yoma 72b.

/4/ Shabbath 116a.

/5/ *Sifre,* Deuteronomy 32:46.

/6/ Shabbath 31a.

/7/ Berakoth 5b.

SEC. 18

/1/ Berakoth 31a.

/2/ Shabbath 30b.

/3/ Berakoth 28b.

/4/ Hullin 122b.

/5/ Berakoth 15a.

/6/ *Ibid.,* 25a.

/7/ *Ibid.*

/8/ *Ibid.,* 23a.

/9/ Megillah 27b.

/10/ *The Zohar,* trans. H. Sperling, M. Simon and P. Levertoff (4 Vols.; London: Soncino Press, 1931-1934), II, 28.

/11/ Berakoth 32b.

/12/ Erubin 64a.

/13/ Berakoth 31a.

/14/ *Ibid.* See also, "Decided laws which admit of no discussion," in Berakoth 31a, *Babylonian Talmud in English,* ed. Isidore Epstein (36 Vols.; London: Soncino Press, 1935-1953), I, 188.

/15/ *Ibid.,* 29b.

/16/ Maimonides, Hilkhoth Tefillah, 1:1.

/17/ Berakoth 30a.

/18/ *Ibid.*

/19/ *Ibid.,* 10b.

/20/ Shabbath 10a.

/21/ *Ibid.*

/22/ Berakoth 10b.

/23/ *Ibid.,* 31a.

/24/ *Ibid.,* 34a.

/25/ *Midrash Rabbah,* ed. H. Freedman and M. Simon (10 Vols.; London: Soncino Press, 1939), Esther, IX, 20.

/26/ Berakoth 12a.

/27/ Berakoth 34b.

/28/ This is the preferred reading. The original read: "He sits on the right and falls on his face" (see Perush).

/29/ This should read "in the laws of idolatry," referring to Maimonides, Hilkhoth Tefillah, 5:14.

/30/ Taanith 14b.

/31/ Abodah Zarah 8a.

/32/ Berakoth 34a.

/33/ *Ibid.,* 14a.

/34/ The Perush states that the words are missing and it should read "and so it is prohibited to extend greetings to a friend before a prayer except in a case where he met him in the street and then it is permissable."

/35/ Berakoth 26b.

/36/ Taanith 27a.

/37/ Shabbath 119b.

/38/ *Tikkune Zohar,* ed. Shamaryahu Zuckerman (Wilna: Fin and Rosenkranz Publisher, 1867), Chapter XVIII, p. 67.

/39/ Shabbath 119b.

/40/ Megillah 28a.

/41/ *Midrash Rabbah,* ed. Soncino, Lamentations, VIII, 13.

/42/ Berakoth 47b.

/43/ Such prayers that require the presence of a quorum, or minyan, which consists of a minimum of ten males over the age of thirteen.

/44/ Eleazar ben Judah of Worms, *Sefer Rokeah* (Zalkwo: 1806), Chapter CCCLXII, p. 81.

/45/ *Daily Prayerbook,* trans. Dr. Joseph Hertz (rev. ed.; New York: Bloch Publishing Co., 1948), p. 151, "We give thanks."

/46/ Berakoth 34b. This refers to the section of the "Eighteen Benedictions," which begins, "Praised be thou, O Lord, God of our fathers, God of Abraham, God of Isaac, God of Jacob." See *Daily Prayer Book,* ed. Hertz, p. 130.

/47/ Berakoth 33b. It would seem that he is addressing two divinities.

/48/ Megillah 24b.

/49/ A group of Psalms read at the beginning of the morning service. See *Daily Prayer Book,* ed. Hertz, p. 50.

/50/ Yebamoth 105b.

/51/ Tosafoth, Berakoth 12b, "Bend like a reed."

SEC. 19

/1/ Maimonides, Hilkhoth Teshuvah, 4:1.

/2/ Repented of the twenty-four items listed here.

/3/ Joseph Albo, *Sefer ha-Ikkarim* (Book of Principles), ed. Isaac Husik (5 Vols.; Philadelphia: Jewish Publication Society, 1946), I, 99.

/4/ "His actions," is the preferred reading.

/5/ Shabbath 54b.

/6/ In the text, "he does not know" is lacking.

/7/ "The thief."

/8/ Baba Metzia 82b.

/9/ Yebamoth 63b; Ben Sira 9:5.

/10/ Baba Bathra 57b.

/11/ Berakoth 24a.

/12/ *Ibid.*

/13/ *Ibid.*

/14/ Abodah Zarah 20b.

/15/ Shabbath 97a.

/16/ *Midrash Rabbah,* ed. Soncino, Ecclesiastes, VIII, 80.

SEC. 20

/1/ Maimonides, Hilkhoth Teshuvah, 1:1.

/2/ Yoma, 84b.

/3/ Sanhedrin 43b.

/4/ *Yalkut Shimoni,* ed. Horeb, Numbers, par. 701, p. 444.

/5/ Lit. "The goat to be sent away." The scapegoat used for the Yom Kippur ritual sent into the wilderness carrying the sins of the people. (See Leviticus 16:8.)

/6/ J. T. Shebuoth 1:6.

/7/ Kiddushin 40b.

/8/ Yoma 85b.

/9/ *Ibid.,* 86a.

/10/ Abodah Zarah 19a.

/11/ Kiddushin 40b.

/12/ *The Zohar,* ed. Soncino, V, 334, 335.

/13/ Rashi, Yoma 21a.

SEC. 21

/1/ The previous chapter instructs him to enumerate his sins. This can be done if he records them. Hence the custom of the pious (Perush).

/2/ Another reason for recording them is to fulfill the demands of the verse.

/3/ Yoma 86b.

/4/ Rosh ha-Shanah 18a.

/5/ Yoma 86b.

SEC. 22

/1/ Yoma 19b; Shabbath 149b.

/2/ Sanhedrin 11a.

/3/ Shebuoth 39a.

/4/ Shabbath 54b.

SEC. 23

/1/ Maimonides, Hilkhoth Teshuvah, 2:9.

/2/ Yoma 85b.

/3/ Baba Kamma 92a.

/4/ Yoma 87b.

/5/ *Ibid.*

/6/ *Midrash Rabbah,* ed. Soncino, Numbers, VI, 772.

/7/ Leviticus 19:18.

SEC. 24

/1/ Yebamoth 79a.

/2/ See II Samuel 21:1, in *Soncino Books of the Bible,* ed. A. Cohen (London: Soncino Press, 1949), 319.

/3/ Yoma 87b.

SEC. 25

/1/ Baba Kamma 103a.

SEC. 26

/1/ Shabbath 153a.

/2/ Aboth 4:22.

SEC. 28

/1/ *Rokeah,* ed. Zalkwo, Chapter XX, p. 9b.

/2/ Shabbath 104a.

/3/ Shebuoth 18a.

/4/ *Shulhan Arukh,* "Orah Hayim," 85:1.

/5/ Kiddushin 30b.

/6/ Shabbath 40b.

/7/ Kiddushin 71b.

SEC. 29

/1/ Aboth 3:14.

/2/ Hagigah 5b.

/3/ Aboth 2:1.

SEC. 30

/1/ Shabbath 105b.

/2/ Genesis 4:7.

/3/ Gittin 57a.

/4/ Baba Metzia 58b.

/5/ Berakoth 18b.

SEC. 31

/1/ Aboth 2:1.

/2/ Abodah Zarah 18a.

/3/ *Ibid.*, 2a.

/4/ Job 7:1.

/5/ Berakoth 28b.

/6/ This refers to the breath of life, actual breathing.

/7/ Aboth 6:4.

/8/ *Ibid.*, 4:28.

/9/ *Ibid.*, 1:12.

/10/ *Ibid.*, 1:6.

/11/ *Ibid.*, 2:9.

SEC. 32

/1/ According to Jewish folklore after the body is placed in the grave it is subjected to violent and painful afflictions.

/2/ Aboth 5:23.

SEC. 33

/1/ Maimonides, Hilkhoth Teshuvah, 5:12

/2/ Berakoth 33b.

/3/ Niddah 16b.

/4/ This world and the next.

SEC. 34

/1/ Arakhin 15a.

/2/ They were sent by Moses to search out the Holy Land. (See Numbers 13 and Deuteronomy 1:22.)

/3/ Maimonides, Hilkhoth Deoth, 2:4.

/4/ Yoma 19b.

/5/ *Ibid.*

/6/ Yebamoth 56b.

/7/ Hagigah 5b.

/8/ Pesahim 3b.

/9/ Aboth 3:17.

/10/ Derekh Eretz Zuta, Chapter II.

SEC. 35

/1/ Lit. "Searcher of kidneys."

/2/ Shabbath 149a.

/3/ *Midrash Rabbah,* ed. Horeb. Genesis, Chapter LXXIII, p. 158a.

SEC. 36

/1/ *Shulhan Arukh,* "Orah Hayim," 1:1, note Isserles.

SEC. 37

/1/ Shabbath 31b.

SEC. 38

/1/ The translation is dubious.

/2/ Gabirol, *Choice of Pearls,* ed. Phillipawski, p. 17.

/3/ Baba Metzia 107b.

––––––––

SEC. 39

/1/ Hullin 89a.

/2/ This is the preferred reading. Words "those whom you know" are not
in text.

––––––––

SEC. 40

/1/ Baba Metzia 58b.

/2/ Berakoth 12b.

––––––––

SEC. 41

/1/ Kiddushin 80b.

––––––––

SEC. 42

/1/ Saadiah Gaon, *The Book of Beliefs and Opinions,* trans. Samuel
Rosenblatt (4th printing; New Haven, Conn: Yale University Press, 1958),
Treatise V, Cahpter V, p. 220.

/2/ Taanith 16a.

/3/ *Pesikta d'Rav Kahana,* ed. Solomon Buber (Wilna: Romm Publisher,
1925), p. 294.

––––––––

SEC. 43

/1/ Berakoth 19a.

/2/ Moed Katan 16a.

/3/ Berakoth 19a.

/4/ Kiddushin 28a.

/5/ Berakoth 19a.

/6/ Baba Kamma 112b.

/7/ *Ibid.,* 112b and 113a.

/8/ *Ibid.,* 15b.

/9/ *Ibid.,* 114a.

/10/ *Ibid.,* 113b.

/11/ Special gifts, such as the breast and shank of peace offerings, were set aside for the priests.

/12/ Hullin 132b.

/13/ Pesahim 52a.

/14/ Betzah 4b.

/15/ Pesahim 50b.

/16/ Nedarim 7b.

/17/ J. T. Moed Katan 3:1.

/18/ Berakoth 19a.

/19/ *Ibid.,* 63a.

/20/ Moed Katan 17a.

/21/ J. T. Moed Katan 3:1.

/22/ Sanhedrin 25a. *Terefah.* Lit. "torn." Term signifies flesh of clean beasts rendered unfit for food as a result of either being mauled or killed by beasts of prey, injured, found defective or unskillfully slaughtered, although in valid fashion.

/23/ Hullin 18a.

/24/ Niddah 13b.

/25/ Ketuboth 28a.

/26/ Moed Katan 17a.

/27/ *Ibid.*

SEC. 44

/1/ Sotah 42a.

/2/ Sanhedrin 102b.

/3/ Maimonides, Commentary on Aboth, Chapter I, p. 16.

/4/ J. T. Baba Kamma 8:7.

/5/ *Midrash Tanhuma* (Berlin: Horeb Publishers, 1924), Pekuday, p. 344.

/6/ Baba Kamma 90a and 91a.

/7/ Hagigah 5a.

/8/ Megillah 28a.

/9/ Hagigah 5a.

/10/ Yoma 19b. The Soncino translation reads: "Whosoever suspects good folks will suffer (for it) on his own body."

/11/ Shabbath 97a.

/12/ Yoma 38a.

/13/ *Shulhan Arukh,* "Hoshen Mishpat," 348.

/14/ Baba Metzia 61b.

/15/ Shabbath 128b.

/16/ The French term for spurs.

SEC. 45

/1/ Berakoth 28b.

/2/ Jeremiah 41:9.

/3/ *Ibid.,* 41.

/4/ I Kings 15:18.

/5/ Niddah 61a.

/6/ Shabbath 32a.

/7/ Berakoth 62b.

/8/ *Yalkut Shimoni,* ed. Horeb, Esther, par. 1054, p. 1057.

SEC. 46

/1/ Aboth 2:17.

/2/ J. T. Sanhedrin 8:7.

/3/ Rosh ha-Shanah 28b.

/4/ *Midrash Rabbah,* ed. Soncino, Exodus, III, 108.

/5/ Nedarim 62a.

/6/ Yoma 38a.

/7/ Nedarim 62a.

/8/ Moed Katan 16b.

/9/ In varying cases the Targum (lit. translation) deals with all or parts of the Bible. It is paraphrastic in nature, bordering between translation and explanation.

/10/ The deeds will be revealed to all souls in heaven.

/11/ Kiddushin 31b.

/12/ *Shulhan Arukh,* "Yoreh Deah," 240:10, Taz, note 13.

SEC. 47

/1/ Horayoth 13a.

/2/ Louis Ginzberg, *Legends of the Jews* (7 Vols.; Philadelphia: Jewish Publications Society, 1909-1938), VII, 299, note 85.

/3/ Shabbath 55a.

/4/ Baba Metzia 49a.

/5/ Shebuoth 31a.

/6/ Baba Metzia 49a.

/7/ Sanhedrin 92a.

/8/ *Ibid.,* 89b.

/9/ Ketuboth 77b.

SEC. 48

/1/ Aboth 4:1.

/2/ *Ibid.,* 4:2.

/3/ Ecclesiastes 1:14.

SEC. 49

/1/ Sanhedrin 58b.

/2/ *Ibid.*

/3/ *Ibid.*

/4/ Makkoth 8a.

/5/ The ordinance of Rabbi Gershom (960-1040) prohibited polygamy among Jews.

/6/ *Mekilta,* ed. Lauterbach, Exodus, III, 32.

SEC. 50

/1/ Derekh Eretz Zuta, Chapter VII.

/2/ *Ibid.,* Chapters III, IV.

/3/ Shabbath 151b.

/4/ The prophet.

/5/ Maimonides, Hilkhoth Deoth, 5:2.

/6/ Gittin 70a. The text emphasizes moderation in eating.

/7/ Berakoth 63a.

SEC. 51

/1/ Pesahim 113b.

/2/ *Aboth of Rabbi Nathan,* ed. Schechter, version A, Chapter XXVIII, p. 86.

/3/ Hullin 94a.

/4/ Tosafoth, Gittin 62a, "Peace to you."

/5/ Berkoth 17a. The wicked were not accorded this deference (see Mekor Hesed).

/6/ *Ibid.,* 7b.

/7/ Daath Zekenim Baale Tosafoth, Deuteronomy 20:10. See also R. Nissen, end of Chapter V, of Gittin.

/8/ *Midrash Rabbah,* ed. Soncino, Genesis 1:303.

/9/ Taanith 23b.

/10/ Hullin 94a.

/11/ Makkoth 24a.

/12/ Aboth 3:17.

/13/ Berakoth 31a.

/14/ Sanhedrin 59b.

/15/ Aboth 1:15.

/16/ *Midrash Rabbah,* ed. Soncino, Numbers, VI, 796.

/17/ Aboth 4:1.

/18/ *Ibid.,* 4:28.

SEC. 52

/1/ Maimonides, Hilkhoth Deoth, 3:1.

/2/ *Tanna debe Eliyahu,* ed. Lector M. Friedman (Vienna: Achiasaf, 1902), Chapter XIV, p. 69.

/3/ Baba Kamma 91b.

/4/ Taanith 11a.

/5/ *Shulhan Arukh,* "Orah Hayim," 288:3.

/6/ Taanith 22b.

/7/ J. T. Demai 7:3.

/8/ Maimonides, Eight Chapters, Chapter IV.

SEC. 53

/1/ Nedarim 32a.

/2/ I Kings 3:11.

/3/ Erubin 54b.

/4/ Berakoth 7a.

/5/ Taanith 11a.

/6/ Sanhedrin 8a.

/7/ *Sifre,* Deuteronomy 1:17.

/8/ Berakoth 28b.

/9/ J. T. Shabbath 1:3.

/10/ Berakoth 43b.

/11/ The French term *prunelle* means pupil of the eye or eyeball.

/12/ Kiddushin 31a.

SEC. 54

/1/ Baba Metzia 58b.

/2/ J. T. Yebamoth 16:3.

/3/ Maimonides, Hilkhoth Teshuvah, 7:8.

/4/ Berakoth 12b.

/5/ *Shulhan Arukh,* "Orah Hayim," 138, see Baer Hetev, note 3.

/6/ Kiddushin 81a.

/7/ Makkoth 12b.

SEC. 55

/1/ Yoma 23a.

/2/ Sotah 5a.

/3/ Berakoth 5a.

SEC. 56

/1/ Shabbath 127a.

/2/ Tosafoth, Hullin 84a, "Ten."

/3/ Ketuboth 111b.

/4/ *Midrash Rabbah,* ed. Horeb, Numbers, Chapter XXI, p. 168.

/5/ Daath Zekenim Baale Tosafoth, Deuteronomy 21:7.

/6/ Sanhedrin 104a.

/7/ Sotah 46b.

/8/ Sanhedrin 103b.

SEC. 57

/1/ Berakoth 25a.

/2/ *Ibid.,* 23a.

/3/ *The Zohar,* ed. Soncino, V, 326; also Shabbath 104a.

/4/ Berakoth 23a.

/5/ *Ibid.,* 15a.

/6/ Shabbath 10a.

/7/ They go uncovered during the week.

SEC. 58

/1/ Berakoth 15a.

/2/ Antlia (Latin)—a machine for drawing water.

/3/ Hullin 105a.

/4/ Hagigah 18b.

/5/ Sotah 4b.

/6/ Berakoth 19a.

/7/ The Perush suggests this reading.

/8/ Shabbath 62b.

/9/ *Tur,* "Orah Hayim," 7, comment of the Beth Yosef.

/10/ *Shulhan Arukh,* "Orah Hayim," 4:22.

/11/ *Ibid.,* 163:1.

/12/ Hullin 106b.

/13/ *Shulhan Arukh,* "Orah Hayim," 157; see Mogen Avraham, note 3.

/14/ Mikwaoth 9:2.

/15/ Moses Premzel, *Mateh Mosheh* (Warsaw: N. Shrifgisser Publisher, 1876), Part IV, Chapter CDXI, p. 103.

/16/ See *Daily Prayerbook,* ed. Hertz, p. 388. The Silent Devotion is followed by the prayer "And the heaven . . . " which is followed in turn by the *Ovos* (Blessed art Thou, God of our fathers) and the *Kaddish* (magnified and sanctified be His great name).

SEC. 59

/1/ Jonah Gerondi, *Sefer ha-Yirah,* ed. Benjamin Silber (Jerusalem: Horeb Publishers, 1952), Chapter CCXXVIII, p. 25a.

/2/ In the event that the fire does not kindle the first time, he is not permitted to go back and take fire a second time. Not eating eggs refers to the rest of the week.

/3/ Toseftah, Shabbath 7:2.

/4/ Abodah Zarah 55a.

/5/ These are negative commandments.

/6/ Daath Zekenim Baale Tosafoth, Genesis 32:33.

/7/ Horayoth 12a.

/8/ Rashi, Yoma 33b.

/9/ The two words share five letters in common. Adding a *vav* to the word *matzos* (unleavened bread) gives us a new Hebrew word meaning "commandments."

/10/ Kiddushin 48a.

SEC. 60

/1/ Yoma 86a.

/2/ Pesahim 54a.

/3/ Sanhedrin 43b.

/4/ Berakoth 34b.

SEC. 61

/1/ Baba Kamma 16b.

/2/ *The Zohar,* ed. Soncino, I, 334.

/3/ Peah 8:5.

/4/ Maimonides, Commentary on Aboth, Chapter III, p. 15.

/5/ Meaning to give to many poor. Erubin 63a.

/6/ Gittin 7b.

/7/ The *perutah* was the smallest copper coin current. See *The Mishnah,* trans. Herbert Danby (London: Oxford Press, 1949), p. 797.

/8/ Baba Bathra 9a.

/9/ Tosafoth, Pesahim 29b.

/10/ Baba Bathra 9b.

/11/ *Midrash Rabbah,* ed. Soncino, Leviticus, IV, 380.

SEC. 62

/1/ Abodah Zarah 19a.

/2/ *Ibid.*

/3/ Aboth 1:3.

/4/ Baba Metziah 107a.

/5/ *Midrash Rabbah,* ed. Soncino, Ecclesiastes, VIII, 7.

SEC. 63

/1/ *Sifre,* Deuteronomy, 11:13.

/2/ The meaning here is that when a person's passions seek to drive him to sin clandestinely, let him reflect upon impure desires ". . . were he before . . . ." (See Perush.)

/3/ Berakoth 28b.

SEC. 64

/1/ Pesahim 118a.

/2/ *Aboth of Rabbi Nathan,* ed. Schechter, Chapter XII, p. 48.

/3/ The Perush suggests we· read, "but he will not tell this to others," since you heard him out and thereby helped to remove the matter from his heart. I don't feel that this emandation is necessary. The original seems to convey a more cogent line of argument.

/4/ Tosafoth, Abodah Zarah, Chapter I.

/5/ Maimonides, Hilkhoth Deoth, 7:4.

/6/ *Midrash Rabbah,* ed. Soncino, Genesis, I, 150, "For every person hates his fellow craftsman."

/7/ Taanith 20b.

/8/ Baba Bathra 21a.

/9/ Kiddushin 70b.

/10/ Niddah 61a.

/11/ Nedarim 10a.

/12/ Temurah 3b.

SEC. 65

/1/ Ketubah 50a.

/2/ Aboth 5:21.

SEC. 66

/1/ Sukkah 29a.

/2/ Taanith 12b.

/3/ See S. H. Bologna (ed.), section 230.

SEC. 67

/1/ Abodah Zarah 5a. The Messiah will not come until all souls will have appeared on earth. Hence, if a person dies without offspring as a result of punishment the Messiah is that much longer delayed. The quicker all souls are born the sooner the Messiah will appear.

/2/ Maimonides, Hilkhoth Talmud Torah, 7:13.

/3/ Shabbath 88b.

/4/ Megillah 28a.

/5/ J. T. Moed Katan 3:1.

/6/ Scholars are worthy of emulation.

/7/ *Shulhan Arukh,* "Yoreh Deah," 242:32, see Isserles' note.

/8/ *Ibid.,* 243:9.

SEC. 68

/1/ Berakoth 31a.

/2/ *The Midrash on Psalms,* trans. William Braude (2 Vols.; New Haven, Conn.: Yale University Press, 1959), II, 147.

/3/ Berakoth 31a.

/4/ Shabbath 30b.

SEC. 69

/1/ Moed Katan 18b.

SEC. 70

/1/ Sanhedrin 14a.

/2/ Pesahim 87b.

/3/ Sotah 13b.

/4/ Pesahim 66b.

SEC. 71

/1/ Shabbath 105b.

SEC. 72

/1/ Ketuboth 5b.

/2/ *Ibid.*, 14b.

SEC. 73

/1/ Baba Metzia 58b.

/2/ Aboth 2:17.

/3/ Ketuboth 11a.

SEC. 74

/1/ This refers to Diocletian who was supposed to have been a swine-herder near Tiberias prior to becoming emperor of Rome. Apparently he was tormented by children and when he was elevated to the purple he sought revenge. See also *Midrash Rabbah,* ed. Horeb, Genesis, Chapter LXIII, p. 132; J. T. Terumoth 8:4.

SEC. 75

/1/ Yoma 19b.

/2/ Aboth 1:5.

/3/ *Ibid.*, 3:18.

SEC. 76

/1/ Berakoth 10a.

/2/ Sanhedrin 48b.

/3/ Pesahim 113b.

/4/ Aboth 4:3.

SEC. 77

/1/ Shabbath 127b.

/2/ Aboth 1:6.

/3/ J. T. Berakoth 9:1.

SEC. 78

/1/ Aboth 4:2.

SEC. 79

/1/ Gabirol, *Choice of Pearls*, ed. Phillipawski, p. 15.

/2/ Sukkah 56b.

/3/ Baba Kamma 92b.

SEC. 80

/1/ *Gabirol, Choice of Pearls*, ed. Phillipowski, p. 22.

/2/ *Ibid.*, p. 17.

/3/ Rashi, Berakoth 8b, "The Field."

/4/ Gabirol, *Choice of Pearls,* ed. Phillipawski, p. 18.

––––––––

SEC. 81

/1/ Rashi, Genesis 8:21. The repetition is tantamount to an oath.

––––––––

SEC. 82

/1/ Aboth 2:15.

––––––––

SEC. 84

/1/ Arakhin 16b.

/2/ Horayoth 13b.

/3/ The commentators, Mekor Hesed and Perush, suggest the following readings: (Perush) "Do not laugh at the mistake . . . mouth. Close your ears . . . to God. Better that you keep silent and let him say etc. . . ." (Mekor Hesed) "Do not laugh at the mistake . . . of your mouth. Better that you keep silent . . . call him sinner. Close your ears to the churl . . . hope to God. If he is an elderly man. . . ."

––––––––

SEC. 85

/1/ Gabirol, *Choice of Pearls,* ed. Phillipawski, p. 16.

/2/ Yoma 4b.

––––––––

SEC. 86

/1/ Aboth 3:17.

/2/ Megillah, 18a.

/3/ Derekh Eretz Zuta, Chapter III.

SEC. 87

/1/ Shabbath 151b.

SEC. 88

/1/ Gabirol, *Choice of Pearls,* ed. Phillipawski, p. 32.

/2/ *Ibid.,* p. 6.

/3/ *Ibid.,* p. 33.

/4/ Derekh Eretz Zuta, Chapter VI.

/5/ Sotah 42a.

/6/ Abodah Zarah 18b.

/7/ Gittin 7a.

/8/ Aboth 2:4.

SEC. 89

/1/ Gabirol, *Choice of Pearls,* ed. Phillipawski, p. 27.

/2/ *Ibid.,* p. 24.

/3/ Text reads "things," preferred reading is "secrets" (Mekor Hesed).

SEC. 90

/1/ Ketuboth 11a.

/2/ Shabbath 10a.

SEC. 91

/1/ Kiddushin 32b.

SEC. 92

/1/ Nedarim 32a.

SEC. 93

/1/ Shebuoth 39a.

/2/ Yoma 38b.

SEC. 95

/1/ Berakoth 54a.

/2/ *Ibid.*, 60a.

/3/ In the "Eighteen Benedictions." See, *Daily Prayer Book,* ed. Hertz, p. 130.

/4/ Berakoth 33b.

/5/ *Ibid.*, 21a.

SEC. 96

/1/ *Ibid.*, 27b.

/2/ Gittin 62a.

SEC. 98

/1/ Derekh Eretz Zuta, Chapter I.

SEC. 99

/1/ Scriptio defectiva.

/2/ Zebahim 118b.

SEC. 100

/1/ Toseftah, Peah, Chapter III.

SEC. 101

/1/ View *infra,* par. 903, warning against the use of holy books for purposes other than study.

SEC. 102

/1/ *Shulhan Arukh,* "Orah Hayim," 167, Mogen Avraham, note 13.

/2/ Hagigah 27a.

/3/ Yebamoth 121b.

/4/ Rashi, Genesis 23:2. The news precipitated her death.

SEC. 103

/1/ Shabbath 32a.

/2/ The Perush suggests that, "Greater is the merit," is the beginning of the next paragraph.

SEC. 104

/1/ Pesahim 113a.

/2/ Aboth 5:26.

/3/ Berakoth 6a.

SEC. 105

/1/ Since nobody busies himself with this particular commandment it is as though it were "dead." Hence his preoccupation with it is regarded as fulfilling the commandment to honor and care for the dead.

/2/ *Midrash Rabbah,* ed. Soncino, Leviticus, IV, 239.

SEC. 106

/1/ Yoma 86a.

/2/ Sanhedrin 44a.

/3/ The letters, when added together, total 248.

/4/ Bekhoroth 45a.

SEC. 107

/1/ J. T. Kiddushin 1:7.

SEC. 109

/1/ Sopherim 3:10.

SEC. 110

/1/ Berakoth 24a.

/2/ *Midrash Tanhuma,* ed. Horeb, Vayera, p. 62.

/3/ J. T. Shabbath 15:3.

/4/ *Ibid.*

SEC. 111

/1/ Hullin 105b.

/2/ Tamid 27b.

SEC. 112

/1/ Maimonides, Hilkhoth Deoth, 6:8.

SEC. 113

/1/ Arakhin 17a.

/2/ Shabbath 33b.

SEC. 114

/1/ J. T. Erubin 3:9.

/2/ This is not the Kalir. It is Samuel the Babylonian.

SEC. 116

/1/ The proselyte.

/2/ Baba Metzia 59b.

/3/ *Midrash Rabbah,* ed. Horeb, Numbers, Chapter VIII, p. 43; also *Midrash Tanhuma,* ed. Horeb, Lech L'cho, p. 52.

SEC. 117

/1/ *Midrash Rabbah,* ed. Horeb, Deuteronomy, Chapter II, p. 8.

SEC. 118

/1/ Yoma 74b.

/2/ Baba Bathra 2b.

SEC. 119

/1/ Erubin 65a.

SEC. 121

/1/ Pesahim 50b.

SEC. 122

/1/ Premzel, *Mateh Mosheh,* ed. Shrifgisser, Part IV, Chapter CDV, p. 103.

SEC. 123

/1/ Baba Bathra 164a.

/2/ Maimonides, Commentary on Aboth, Chapter I, p. 3.

/3/ Berakoth 54a. Another possible meaning is that one should love God no matter what treatment he metes out, good or evil.

/4/ Erubin 22a.

SEC. 124

/1/ Lit. Honi The Circle-Drawer. See *Jewish Encyclopedia,* IX, 404, for a full treatment of the person and his reputed powers. He was regarded as a miracle worker. During a drought he prayed for rain by drawing a circle, entering it, and refusing to step out until his prayers were answered.

/2/ Taanith 23a.

SEC. 125

/1/ Peah 8:9.

/2/ Ketuboth 68a.

SEC. 126

/1/ Sotah 21b.

/2/ Yoma 22b.

/3/ I Kings 20:36.

SEC. 127

/1/ Maimonides, Hilkhoth Deoth, 4:1.

/2/ Makkoth 15b.

/3/ Tamid 27b.

SEC. 128

/1/ Berakoth 63b.

SEC. 129

/1/ Rashi, Proverbs 3:9.

/2/ Shabbath 133b.

SEC. 130

/1/ *Ibid.*

/2/ Berakoth 32b.

SEC. 132

/1/ Ahitophel, who was asked to advise, gave advice congenial to the desires of Absalom but contrary to God's will. Later Hushai gave counsel in keeping with God's will but contrary to the desires of Absalom. As a result of Hushai's advice Absalom fell into David's hands. However, if Hushai had remained silent, Absalom would have followed Ahitophel's advice (Perush).

SEC. 133

/1/ Yoma 19b.

SEC. 134

/1/ Proverbs 25:21-22.

SEC. 135

/1/ Berakoth 8a.

/2/ Baba Metzia 59a.

/3/ *Ibid.*, 87a.

/4/ *Ibid.*, 59a.

SEC. 137

/1/ J. T. Berakoth 9:2.

/2/ Berakoth 30b.

SEC. 138

/1/ *Midrash Rabbah,* ed. Horeb, Exodus, Chapter XLIII, p. 100.

/2/ Shabbath 87a.

SEC. 139

/1/ J. T. Hagigah 2:1.

SEC. 140

/1/ *Midrash Rabbah,* ed. Horeb, Numbers, Chapter XX, p. 161.

SEC. 141

/1/ Megillah 27a.

/2/ A tale or just ordinary secular writings.

SEC. 143

/1/ Sanhedrin 45b.

SEC. 144

/1/ Taanith 9a.

/2/ Valuables that he had given up for lost.

/3/ The words "whole tithe" is taken to imply all sorts of revenue accruing from all sources, foreseen and unforeseen. (Perush.)

/4/ The Bible does not mention income from interest since it was then not prevalent.

/5/ Berakoth 63a.

SEC. 145

/1/ Taanith 4a.

/2/ J. T. Taanith 3:11.

/3/ Pesahim 113b.

/4/ Nedarim 22a.

/5/ Kiddushin 41a.

/6/ Nedarim 22b.

/7/ Shabbath 30b.

/8/ Gittin 6b.

/9/ Rosh ha-Shanah 17a.

/10/ Maimonides, Hilkhoth Teshuvah, 3:6.

SEC. 147

/1/ The accents and notations for cantillating the Biblical Text.

/2/ Megillah 32a.

/3/ Sanhedrin 101a.

/4/ Kiddushin 30a. Five thousand five hundred sentences would be nearer the true total. It is possible that a *heh* denoting five thousand instead of a *het* denoting eight thousand, was intended. None the less, the figure is only approximate.

/5/ As a result of repeated interruptions they have intensified the division.

SEC. 148

/1/ J. T. Shabbath 1:2.

/2/ Ketuboth 5b.

SEC. 149

/1/ Abodah Zarah 3a.

/2/ Baba Kamma 32b.

/3/ Isaiah 58:13.

/4/ Shabbath 119a.

SEC. 150

/1/ Erubin 41a.

/2/ *Shulhan Arukh,* "Orah Hayim," 249, Mogen Avraham, note 7.

/3/ Word "obligatory" is inserted for a preferred reading (Perush).

SEC. 151

/1/ Shabbath 116a.

SEC. 152

/1/ J. T. Peah 1:1.

/2/ Kiddushin 31b.

/3/ *Ibid.,* 32a.

SEC. 153

/1/ Berakoth 17a.

/2/ Moses Maimonides, *Guide for the Perplexed,* trans. M. Friedlander (reprint of 1st ed., 1881-1885; New York: Hebrew Publishing Co.), Part 3, Chapter XVII, p. 73.

/3/ *Yalkut Reuveni* (Warsaw: Levin and Epstein Publishers), Numbers, Chapter II, pp. 118-119.

/4/ Sanhedrin 68a.

/5/ I Kings 2:40.

/6/ Shabbath 55a.

/7/ Ecclesiastes 12:12.

SEC. 154

/1/ These are the categories of work prohibited on the Sabbath.

/2/ *Daily Prayer Book* (Hertz), p. 390.

/3/ See *The Mishnah,* ed. Danby, p. 793. The *Erub* (lit. mixture, amalgamation or combination) is used to extend the movements of an individual on the Sabbath beyond the two thousand cubit limitation imposed upon him by law. The precise formulation and application of the *Erub* is the subject of the tractate Erubin.

/4/ Betzah 36b.

SEC. 155

/1/ (Perush.) This is the preferred sequence. In the original text the first verse "the beginning of wisdom" appears later.

/2/ Aboth 2:1.

/3/ J. T. Yoma 1:1, also *Midrash Rabbah,* ed. Horeb, Leviticus, Chapter XXVI, p. 69.

/4/ "She" refers to Torah.

/5/ This is a paraphrase of Proverbs 6:22.

/6/ Berakoth 60b.

/7/ Yoma 77b.

/8/ Yebamoth 120a.

/9/ They don't know if they will succeed.

/10/ This is the preferred reading. (See Mekor Hesed, note 10.)

/11/ "I need to be cunning."

/12/ *Sifra,* ed. Weiss, p. 99b.

/13/ Baba Kamma 38a.

/14/ Used here in the sense "to act wrongly."

/15/ *Midrash Rabbah,* ed. Horeb, Song of Songs, Chapter I, p. 11.

/16/ For there is no evil inclinations.

/17/ *Midrash Rabbah,* ed. Horeb, Ecclesiastes, Chapter XII, p. 128.

/18/ Baba Metzia 32b.

/19/ Menahoth 43b.

/20/ Sanhedrin 74a.

/21/ Toseftah, Baba Kamma, Chapter VII.

/22/ Berakoth 12b.

/23/ Kiddushin 81a.

/24/ II Kings 25:7.

/25/ The letter appears both in the verse from Isaiah and in the verse from Deuteronomy. The letter *kof* has two forms, one is a final letter used at the end of a word, the other is for initial and medial use. The *kof* in the verse from Isaiah begins the quotation and is the initial letter for the word "all." The *kof* in medial form appears in the last word which concludes the quotation from Deuteronomy. Here again the word is "all."

/26/ i.e., into the hands of his sons, daughters, and relatives.

/27/ Ketuboth 50a.

/28/ *Ibid.*, 49a.

SEC. 156

/1/ Baba Metziah 85a.

/2/ *Midrash Rabbah,* ed. Horeb, Ecclesiastes, Chapter IV, p. 91.

/3/ These three virtues correspond to the "three fold chord" of the verse.

/4/ Although found in the text it is repetitive, nevertheless we left it but in parenthesis.

/5/ Berakoth 17b.

SEC. 157

/1/ Aboth 4:8.

/2/ *Midrash Tanhuma,* ed. Horeb, Vayigash, p. 140.

/3/ *Shulhan Arukh,* "Orah Hayim" 76. Mogen Avraham, note 7.

/4/ The Perush states that the three commands are: to meditate on Torah; to pray; to speak to friends only of Godly matters. The two purifications are directives to abstain from the aforementioned commands when he finds himself in a place of filth or if his person is soiled with semen.

/5/ Berakoth 24b.

SEC. 158

/1/ The first three of the eighteen verses dealing with God-fearing are missing. The Perush suggests that the following verses be included: (1) The fear of the Lord is the beginning of knowledge (Prov. 1:7). (2) And did not choose the fear of the Lord (Prov. 1:29). (3) Then shalt thou understand the fear of the Lord (Prov. 2:5).

/2/ Hullin 42a. *Terefah,* Lit., torn. The term signifies flesh of clean beasts rendered unfit for food as a result of either being mauled or killed by beasts of prey, injured, found defective or unskillfully slaughtered although in valid fashion.

/3/ Berakoth 61b.

/4/ Numerical value of the Hebrew word "living" is eighteen.

/5/ Hullin 42a.

/6/ "Fear" in Proverbs stands in apposition to the blessing against the heretics in the "Eighteen Benedictions." This makes for Nineteen Benedictions! See Daily Prayer Book, ed. Hertz, p. 143.

/7/ Berakoth 30b.

/8/ *Ibid.,* 29b.

/9/ J. T. Berakoth 1:1.

/10/ Rosh ha-Shanah 35a.

/11/ *Daily Prayer Book,* ed. Hertz, p. 141.

/12/ *Ibid.,* p. 140.

/13/ Erubin 65a.

/14/ Berakoth 34b.

/15/ *Daily Prayer Book,* ed. Hertz, p. 148.

/16/ Sanhedrin 44b.

/17/ Berakoth 29b.

/18/ See *S. H. Bologna,* Section 171.

/19/ The Hebrew word "to learn" shares a common root with the letter *Lamed.*

/20/ Height-wise, *lamed* is taller than all other letters.

SEC. 159

/1/ Each contains references to wisdom and God-fearing.

/2/ J. T. Terumoth 8:4.

/3/ *Midrash Rabbah,* ed. Horeb, Leviticus, Chapter XXX, p. 81a.

SEC. 160

/1/ *Midrash Rabbah,* ed. Horeb, Genesis, Chapter LII, p. 110.

/2/ *Midrash Rabbah,* ed. Horeb, Leviticus, Chapter XXXII, p. 88.

/3/ See Perush.

/4/ And do not sin.

/5/ Kiddushin 30b.

SEC. 161

/1/ Aboth 2:5.

/2/ Megillah 14b.

/3/ Berakoth 62b.

/4/ He allowed no one to strike Saul.

/5/ Shabbath 56a.

/6/ The *lamed* is used as an acrostic. The "l," "m" and "d" serve as the first letters for each of the three words that comprise the passage.

INDEX OF BIBLICAL REFERENCES

151

155

INDEX